YOU SMELL!!!

# VIETNAM

# VIETNAM
## FOUR AMERICAN PERSPECTIVES

*LECTURES BY*

GEORGE S. MCGOVERN

WILLIAM C. WESTMORELAND

EDWARD N. LUTTWAK

THOMAS J. MCCORMICK

*Edited with an Introduction*
*by Patrick J. Hearden*

*Foreword by Akira Iriye*

PURDUE UNIVERSITY PRESS
WEST LAFAYETTE, INDIANA

**Library of Congress Cataloging-in-Publication Data**

Vietnam : four American perspectives : lectures / by
George S. McGovern . . . [et al.] : edited with an
introduction by Patrick J. Hearden : foreword by
Akira Iriye.
          p.          cm.
ISBN 1–55753–002–5 (alk. paper):
—ISBN 1–55753–003–3 (pbk.) (alk. paper):
        1. Vietnamese Conflict (1961–1975)—United
States. 2. United States—History—1945– I. McGovern,
George S. (George Stanley), 1922– . II. Hearden,
Patrick J., 1942–
DS558.V48 1990                              89–24267
959.704'3373—dc20

*Book and cover designed by James McCammack*

PRINTED IN THE UNITED STATES OF AMERICA

# CONTENTS

FOREWORD
*Akira Iriye*                                                    vii

ACKNOWLEDGMENTS                                                   xi

INTRODUCTION
*Patrick J. Hearden*                                              1

ONE  AMERICA IN VIETNAM
     *George S. McGovern*                                        11

TWO  VIETNAM IN PERSPECTIVE
     *William C. Westmoreland*                                   37

THREE  THE IMPACT OF VIETNAM ON STRATEGIC
       THINKING IN THE UNITED STATES
       *Edward N. Luttwak*                                       59

FOUR  AMERICAN HEGEMONY AND
      THE ROOTS OF THE VIETNAM WAR
      *Thomas J. McCormick*                                      81

INDEX                                                           109

# FOREWORD

## by Akira Iriye

As we near the end of the 1980s and look ahead to the world of the 1990s, the Vietnam War holds particular significance. Recently much has been written of the "decline" of the United States. As popularized by Paul Kennedy's best-selling *Rise and Fall of the Great Powers*, the thesis contends that America's "imperial overstretch" after the Second World War has resulted in a loss of competitiveness and a relative decline in its overall position in the world. By multiplying its global commitments that went beyond a capacity to finance them, and especially by engaging in overseas military activities that drained resources away from domestic needs, so it is often argued, the nation in time broke the precarious balance between ends and means to the detriment of its overall power. The result, according to this view, has been the relative decline of America, similar to the stories of other great powers that have also risen, overextended themselves, and ultimately declined.

Whether the nation is likely to repeat the experiences of others and enter a period of relative decline is a fascinating question that has attracted the attention of a large number of officials, commentators, and the general public. Although no consensus has emerged, the existence of the debate itself is an indication of a profound transformation in America's international relations. It shows that many are convinced that both the world and the nation have changed significantly in recent years, and that regardless of whether or not the United States has entered a period of decline, serious questions need to be raised concerning its role in international affairs at the end of the twentieth century.

In discussing the alleged decline of the nation or in denying such a trend, Kennedy and his critics have paid close attention to the Vietnam War. This is inevitable, given the war's costs, both in monetary and human terms. The war did bring about large-scale governmental deficits; it did trigger an inflationary trend at home; and it did cause the hitherto undisputed dominance of the dollar to be questioned in the international market. All these consequences had the effect of eroding the economic health of the country, which in the 1970s came to be characterized by balance of trade deficits for the first time since the turn of the century, and in the 1980s by huge amounts of foreign borrowing, turning the United States into a net debtor nation for the first time since the First World War.

Whether these developments mean America's "decline," however, has been disputed. While some, following Kennedy, have insisted that the primary objective for the United States now should be to redefine priorities and concentrate on domestic economic reconstruction so as to regain competitiveness, many have contended that thanks to America's military presence in Vietnam, the rest of the region gained much valuable time as it transformed itself into an area of relative stability and prosperity. Others have asserted that American willingness to defend the balance of power, even at the expense of budgetary deficits and monetary indebtedness, has contributed to convincing potential adversaries like the Soviet Union and China of the wisdom of seeking an understanding with the United States. In such a perspective, it would be folly to reduce drastically American global commitments, for the world still counts on the United States to uphold a balance of power.

Thus the current debate on America's relative position in the world reflects a profound impact of the Vietnam War. One's views on the war affect one's thinking on the present and on the larger question of the role the United States should play in the world in the coming years. The four lectures reprinted in this volume offer valuable insights as we sort out many themes and try to develop fresh ideas on international affairs.

The lectures, however, become even more valuable if we keep in mind two additional perspectives. First, we should not forget the war's impact on other countries' perceptions of the United States. Not just the Vietnamese but also the people and governments of all other countries became involved, directly or indirectly, in the conflict and in the process developed their attitudes toward America. And here it will be useful to recall that even some of the nation's staunchest allies, like Great Britain, as well as neutral nations whose support the United States was seeking, such as India and Egypt, grew profoundly disturbed by the escalation of the war. A nation's "rise" or "fall" is, after all, in part a function of how it is perceived by others, and there seems little doubt that the war estranged many countries from the United States.

On the other hand, the Vietnam War also showed how a democracy comes to terms with its own leadership. This is the second perspective we need to keep in mind as we read these lectures. How does a democracy fight a war? Would a democratic nation "decline" as predictably as the autocratic empires of the past as a result of foreign engagements? One of the most notable developments during the war was the revitalization of dissent in America, which may have served to reaffirm the people's faith in the democratic process. And it may have been this aspect of the war that has had a major impact on the rest of the world. American political and intellectual influence has certainly not declined. If anything, it may have continued to grow since the 1960s. Certainly, there is a larger influx of refugees, immigrants, foreign scholars and students, and "undocumented" aliens into the United States than anywhere else in the world, indicating that freedom, intellectual openness, and human rights, which the domestic debate during the war reaffirmed, attract other peoples to America. Abroad, it is interesting to note that since the withdrawal of American forces from Vietnam in 1975, democratic movements have gained momentum in Poland, the Soviet Union, China, and many other countries. To that extent, the war's end cannot be said to have resulted in America's "decline."

So the picture is a complex one. That is as it should be. World affairs need to be looked at in strategic, economic, political, and intellectual frameworks. Those who would understand the forces that will define the world of the 1990s and beyond would do well to relate the manifold experiences of the Vietnam War to the present debate on the rise and fall of the great powers. From an extensive investigation of the relationship between the two will come a fresh understanding that will be of importance not only to the American people but to the rest of the world.

# ACKNOWLEDGMENTS

I want to thank several members of the academic community at Purdue University for helping make the 1987 Louis Martin Sears Lecture series a great success. Lorna Myers and her staff in Convocations and Lectures did a wonderful job in publicizing the affair. Serving as my colleagues on the Sears Lecture Committee, Robert E. May and Laird Kleine-Ahlbrandt helped arrange auditoriums and host receptions for our featured speakers. The Department of History secretaries, working under the supervision of Judy J. McHenry, performed the difficult task of converting the tape recordings of the four public addresses into typewritten copy. Vice Presidnt Varro E. Tyler, Professor Leon E. Trachtman, Dean David A. Caputo of the School of Liberal Arts, and Professor John J. Contreni introduced our guest lecturers. As the head of the history department, Professor Contreni also worked closely with me in planning and overseeing the entire program.

On behalf of the students and faculty at Purdue University, I wish to give special thanks to Senator George S. McGovern, General William C. Westmoreland, Edward N. Luttwak, and Thomas J. McCormick not only for delivering lively addresses and fielding provocative questions but also for making themselves available for personal interviews with news reporters covering the event.

PATRICK J. HEARDEN, Chair
Sears Lecture Committee

# INTRODUCTION

## by Patrick J. Hearden

The following four essays on the subject of America in Vietnam were presented in the spring of 1987 as public addresses for
the Louis Martin Sears Lecture series at Purdue University. The
program was made possible by a grant provided by Professor Sears
after a distinguished career of teaching and research at Purdue in
the field of American diplomatic history. Sears left instructions
that his bequest should be used to educate future generations of
Purdue students about the role that the United States has played in
world affairs. Acting upon his wishes, the Department of History
and Convocations and Lectures invited four experts to the Purdue
campus to speak about different dimensions of the American involvement in the Vietnam War.

In recent years, there has been a ground swell of interest in
the Vietnam War among college students across the United States.
The great majority of these students were not yet born when
American combat troops began fighting in the distant jungles and
rice paddies of Southeast Asia. But many of them have heard stories about relatives and neighbors who were either killed or
wounded while engaging in military operations in Vietnam. And
almost all of them are curious about the antiwar movement, which
disrupted academic life and provoked heated controversy in com-
munities throughout the United States. As their interest in the
Vietnam War intensified, university students raised several key
questions: Why did the United States become involved in the conflict in Southeast Asia? How did American military leaders and
foot soldiers conduct themselves during the struggle? What drove
American political leaders to sustain the war effort? Why did the
United States fail to accomplish its objectives? How has the military defeat affected American foreign policy? What lessons can be
learned from the frustrating experience? In an effort to find an-
swers to these questions, large numbers of students at small liberal

arts colleges as well as huge universities have elected to enroll in courses dealing with various aspects of the Vietnam War.

The Purdue Department of History responded to this mounting interest in two ways. First, the department head asked me to develop an undergraduate lecture course on the involvement of the United States in Southeast Asian affairs to supplement the sequence of general courses that I teach in the field of American diplomacy. Second, the department head appointed me to chair the Sears Lecture Committee with the understanding that my colleagues and I would make preparations for a series of public addresses devoted to the topic of America in Vietnam. We set about our task with great enthusiasm. Realizing that more than a decade had passed since the fall of Saigon, we believed that the time had come to reflect with some detachment and hindsight on the longest war in the history of the United States.

The Sears Lecture Committee sought to put together a balanced program featuring speakers who hold conflicting opinions about the Vietnam War. Two of the speakers chosen by the committee played a direct part in the great debate provoked by America's escalating military intervention in Southeast Asia. One served as the commander of the American military forces in Vietnam until the growing battlefield casualties and economic costs prompted a reappraisal of the attrition strategy employed by the United States. The other ran as the Democratic candidate for president in 1972 on a platform that promised the withdrawal of American soldiers from Indochina. To round out the program, the committee selected two speakers who have reappraised the American entanglement in Vietnam in scholarly publications. One is a strong advocate for military reform in the United States and a frequent participant in high-level government discussions about American strategic interests. The other is a distinguished professor of diplomatic history and an astute critic of American foreign policy.

The first speaker, Senator George S. McGovern, analyzes the actions of the United States in Southeast Asia from the viewpoint of an American citizen concerned about the problem of morality in international relations. In his eyes, the Vietnam War was a great tragedy. McGovern does not question the motives of American statesmen who advocated intervention in Indochina. Nor does he criticize the conduct of American soldiers who were ordered to fight in Vietnam. Yet McGovern finds that the United States was guilty of committing terrible crimes in Southeast Asia despite having honorable intentions. Good men did bad things, he argues, because they were ignorant. After asserting that American leaders did not possess an adequate understanding of Vietnamese history, he concludes that their lack of historical knowledge led them to make a number of grave political, military, and ethical mistakes in Indochina.

According to McGovern, the first great mistake that the United States made in Southeast Asia occurred shortly after the Second World War when President Harry S. Truman decided to help the French reestablish control over their Indochina empire. He points out that during the war, Ho Chi Minh and his guerrilla forces helped rescue American airmen downed in Indochina and that following the conflict, the Vietnamese rebels asked the United States to support their struggle to gain independence from the clutches of French imperialism. But American leaders knew that Ho Chi Minh was a communist, and McGovern argues that they assumed that all communists took their orders from Moscow or Beijing. Claiming that American policymakers were simply unaware of the fact that the Vietnamese have a deep historical hatred for the Chinese, he observes that despite their own revolutionary heritage, the American people found themselves helping the French regain control of their colonial possessions in Indochina.

Senator McGovern believes that the second major American mistake in Southeast Asia occurred after the Geneva Conference in 1954 when President Dwight D. Eisenhower helped block free elections to decide the future of Vietnam. Eisenhower and his advisers feared that, if the elections were held on schedule, Ho Chi Minh would score a landslide victory and that Vietnam would be reunified under communist rule. According to McGovern, American leaders misapplied the historical lesson of Munich to the situation in Indochina and thereby viewed the conflict in South Vietnam as aggression from North Vietnam rather than as a civil war or a social revolution within a single country. He therefore charges that American policymakers were willing to violate the democratic principle of national self-determination in order to build up South Vietnam as a bastion against the spread of communism in Southeast Asia.

McGovern laments that the United States brought great misery to the people of Indochina in the name of promoting freedom in Southeast Asia. While American ground troops had a hard time distinguishing friend from foe in the jungles and rice paddies of Vietnam, American bombs and artillery did not always accurately discriminate between enemy forces and innocent civilians.

Thus the American military methods not only failed to win the hearts and minds of the Vietnamese people, but the widespread death and destruction in Vietnam also haunted American soldiers in the heat of battle and troubled the conscience of people throughout the United States. McGovern takes direct issue with those who assert that the American military endeavor in Vietnam bought time for neighboring countries in Southeast Asia to strengthen themselves against the threat of communism. On the contrary, McGovern charges that the secret American bombing of Cambodia set the stage for the rise of Pol Pot and a communist reign of terror over the Cambodian people.

To complete his condemnation of American policymakers, McGovern complains that the Vietnam War had terrible consequences for the United States as well as Indochina. The American military escalation in Vietnam led to heightened tension between the United States and the Soviet Union, generated chronic inflation in the United States, and undermined the social welfare programs that President Lyndon B. Johnson sponsored under the Great Society banner. The gap between the rhetoric of American leaders and the realities of Vietnam made matters worse by dividing and confusing the people of the United States. After charging that American leaders were willing to sacrifice free speech in the United States in the name of promoting democracy in Vietnam, McGovern suggests that in his determination to stifle domestic dissent, President Richard M. Nixon sowed the seeds for the Watergate scandal, which shortened his term in the White House.

The second speaker, General William C. Westmoreland, analyzes the role of the United States in the Vietnam War from a traditional Cold War perspective. He bases his argument upon the central assumption that ever since the Second World War the entire planet has been divided into the forces of good and evil. On one side, the United States stands at the head of a group of democratic countries that are determined to preserve their liberal institutions. On the other side, the Soviet Union leads a bloc of communist nations that are bent on spreading totalitarian forms of government through the use of violence. Convinced that the United States has a moral responsibility to defend the free world from either internal subversion or external aggression, Westmoreland concludes that American leaders must be prepared to meet the communist challenge with military power.

General Westmoreland begins his address by explaining that the United States had a clear objective in Southeast Asia: to preserve the territorial integrity and political independence of South

Vietnam. In his eyes, this mission grew out of an American determination to resist Russian attempts to grab as much real estate as possible in the aftermath of the Second World War. Citing the pledge made in 1947 by President Truman that the United States would aid free people threatened by subjugation, he argues that American leaders applied the Truman Doctrine to the situation in Indochina. Westmoreland regards the struggle among the Vietnamese people not as a civil war or a social revolution occurring within the confines of one country but rather as an aggressive effort by the communist dictators in North Vietnam to extend their control over the population of South Vietnam. Thus he sees the American commitment to defend South Vietnam as part of the bipartisan United States policy of containing the spread of communism throughout the world.

After defining the American objective in Southeast Asia in these terms, Westmoreland asserts that the United States possessed sufficient military strength to assure the survival of South Vietnam as an independent noncommunist nation. He notes that American troops were equipped with excellent weapons, including helicopters, which gave them unprecedented mobility in a rugged country containing few roads. He also points out that American soldiers were trained in appropriate ways, including counterinsurgency techniques, which enhanced their effectiveness against guerrilla forces. Westmoreland does not disguise his pride in the fact that the men who fought under his command in Indochina never suffered a major defeat comparable to the French disaster at Dien Bien Phu. Nor does he forgo the chance to remind his audience that American combat troops were withdrawn from the battlefield two years before the North Vietnamese army conquered South Vietnam.

General Westmoreland criticizes political leaders in Washington for tying the hands of American military commanders who were directly responsible for the conduct of the war in Indochina. He complains that American ground forces were not allowed to pursue the enemy into Cambodia and Laos and that restraints were imposed upon the use of American air power against North Vietnam. Westmoreland argues that the enemy suffered severe losses during the Tet Offensive in 1968 and that the United States missed a great opportunity to strike while the Vietcong were demoralized. At that time, Westmoreland recalls, he wanted to get authority to send American troops into Cambodia to cut communist supply routes, to make an amphibious and airborne assault above the Demilitarized Zone, and to intensify the bombardment of North Vietnam. Westmoreland laments that President Johnson refused to grant him permission to execute an appropriate strategy that he feels would have forced the enemy to come to the conference table and sue for peace.

But Westmoreland directs his bitterest barbs at news reporters in the United States for undermining public support for the American war effort in Indochina. He charges that irresponsible journalists seriously misled the American people by inaccurately portraying the Tet Offensive as an enemy victory rather than a defeat. Westmoreland likewise blasts news commentators for giving the American people the impression that President Johnson decided not to run for reelection after Tet because the United States was losing the war. Noting that the conflict in Vietnam was the first war covered by television, he suggests that CBS anchorman Walter Cronkite had more influence than President Johnson on how the American public viewed events in Southeast Asia. Westmoreland regrets most of all that government censorship did not prevent the American media from weakening the national resolve to back the war effort until the United States achieved its goals in Vietnam.

After blaming American politicians and news reporters for what went wrong in Indochina, Westmoreland ends on a positive note by suggesting that the men who served under him in Vietnam did not fight in vain. He points out that while the countries under communist domination in Indochina have remained impoverished, the noncommunist nations elsewhere in Southeast Asia have made great strides toward achieving prosperity. Westmoreland claims that by fighting in Indochina against the spread of communism, the United States bought ten years for the people living in the rest of Southeast Asia to develop their own economies and to gain confidence in running their own political affairs. He concludes, therefore, that in the long stretch of history, American actions in Southeast Asia might appear more like a noble victory than a humiliating defeat.

The third speaker, Edward N. Luttwak, analyzes the military behavior of the United States during the Vietnam War from the viewpoint of a sophisticated strategic thinker. Uninterested in making value judgments about the motives underlying the deployment of American military forces around the world, he devotes his attention to studying the strategic position of the United States in the international arena. Luttwak offers neither a criticism nor an apology for the fact that the United States became involved in hostilities in Indochina. Rather than asking why policymakers in Washington decided to send American combat troops to Southeast

Asia, he focuses upon the question of how the United States military establishment went about the business of trying to win the Vietnam War.

Luttwak begins his talk by discussing the complex nature of strategic thinking. He points out that there are four different levels of military strategy: the technical level involving machines, equipment, and weapons; the tactical level involving the maneuvers of small units on the battlefield; the operational level involving multiple troop deployments; and the theater level involving a whole array of forces engaged in combat. Emphasizing the difficulties encountered by those who practice the art of war, Luttwak explains that a nation must be at least adequate on each of these four levels of strategy in order to win a conflict. To complete his analytic framework, he adds that standing above all such military considerations is the level of grand strategy involving political choice. Hence he notes that the military actions of governments may be influenced by both economic and diplomatic concerns.

In contrast to General Westmoreland, Luttwak places the major responsibility for the American defeat in Vietnam squarely upon the shoulders of the United States military command. Luttwak says that it is misleading for Westmoreland to boast that American soldiers never suffered a significant defeat in Vietnam because, as a matter of fact, the United States ultimately abandoned a country that it promised to protect. While agreeing with Westmoreland that American journalists undermined the war effort on the home front, he argues that the United States lost the war in Vietnam primarily because its conduct on the battlefield was not guided by strategic thinking. Luttwak asserts that American military forces in Vietnam engaged in a large number of activities that were either counterproductive or simply irrelevant. Claiming that Westmoreland never really demanded authority from political leaders in Washington to invade North Vietnam, he charges that Westmoreland failed to develop a conceptual method for winning the war and assuring the survival of South Vietnam as a separate noncommunist country.

But Luttwak aims his most biting criticism at the civilians who worked in the Pentagon during the Vietnam War. He denounces Secretary of Defense Robert S. McNamara for allowing the army to rotate officers out of Vietnam after a brief tour of duty to give as many officers as possible a chance to command men in battle and thereby to advance their careers in the military. Due to the frequent rotation of officers, Luttwak charges, the same mistakes were made over and over again on the tactical level in Vietnam. He also castigates McNamara for using the latest methods of business management to run the Defense Department. The efficiency experts who worked under McNamara, laments Luttwak, employed linear logic, which assumes that if any given weapon or maneuver succeeds in the beginning it will continue to do so. He asserts that their failure to understand that every successful military action provokes an enemy countermeasure led to many instances of a misapplication of efficiency by American forces in Vietnam.

Luttwak ends his address with the comforting thought that strategic thinking in the United States has undergone a revival since the close of the Vietnam War. American military experts, he maintains, are now aware of the fact that what works in civilian life does not always work in the realm of strategy. Luttwak likewise intimates that these same military experts also realize the inherent difficulty in the need to succeed at every level of strategic activity in order to defeat an enemy in battle. Although he acknowledges that the United States will not be able to avoid making at least some mistakes during conflicts in the future, Luttwak assures his audience that American military leaders are no longer programmed to fail because they now understand the necessity to think in strategic terms.

The fourth speaker, Thomas J. McCormick, analyzes the American military intervention in Vietnam from the perspective of a scholar concerned with the problem of historical causation. McCormick does not assume that the United States has acted any better or any worse than other nations in the course of history. Nor does he attempt to find scapegoats in the United States to blame for the American failure in Vietnam. Rather than asking whether the war could have been waged differently with different results, McCormick focuses his attention upon the question of why the United States became involved in Vietnam in the first place and why the United States continued to shoulder the burden of the war for so long. Without an understanding of the reasons American leaders were willing to pay the terrible costs of combat in Vietnam, he cautions, it is impossible to speculate about the issue of whether the national interests of the United States justified the payment of yet higher costs in an effort to achieve a victory.

McCormick begins his address by discussing the concept of hegemony in world affairs. Noting that the United States emerged from the Second World War as the dominant power on the international scene, he argues that American leaders were determined to establish a liberal capitalist world system based upon the principle of equal economic opportunity. McCormick maintains that American policymakers aimed to use their preponderance of financial and military power to promote the practice of free trade on a world-wide basis and to protect the new international order against the scourges of revolution and aggression. Observing that government officials and business executives in the United States hoped to replace the Pax Britannica with a Pax Americana, he asserts that they believed that the preservation of free enterprise in the United States depended upon the exportation of surplus American capital and commodities to open markets around the globe.

McCormick explains the American war effort in Vietnam in terms of the hegemonic responsibility of the United States to safeguard the liberal capitalist world system. The original American commitment made in 1950 to pacify Vietnam, he argues, grew out of a determination in Washington to integrate Japan into the new international order devoted to the doctrine of free trade. According to McCormick, policymakers in the United States feared two possible developments: that a successful anticapitalist revolution in Vietnam might have a domino effect on neighboring countries threatened by radical movements; and that Japan might be drawn into a state trading bloc revolving around the People's Republic of China if it did not have access to noncommunist markets in Southeast Asia. McCormick emphasizes that concern about Japan remained the principal motivation underlying the American military involvement in Vietnam until the mid-1960s. But he also explains that the American commitment to prevent the triumph of communism in Vietnam was reinforced by a desire to preserve the credibility of the United States, to discourage revolutionary upheavals elsewhere in the third world, and to save the face of successive occupants of the White House.

McCormick then assesses the consequences of the American military campaign in Indochina. On the one hand, he observes that the United States failed to prevent the loss of Vietnam, Laos, and Cambodia to the forces of communism. McCormick adds that revolutionary groups have continued to destabilize underdeveloped areas and that the ability of the United States to run the world has come to be questioned. On the other hand, he calls attention to the fact that the major "dominoes" in Southeast Asia have not yet fallen under the sway of communism. McCormick points out in a similar vein that Japan has continued to operate in the liberal international trading network and that even China has opted for a partial return to the capitalist system. In contrast to Westmoreland, however, he suggests that most of Southeast Asia might have remained within the capitalist orbit even if the United States had not fought in Indochina.

After acknowledging that the Vietnam War helped produce an erosion of American authority around the globe, McCormick ends his talk by observing that centrifugal tendencies in the world system have stimulated an intense debate among policymakers in the United States. He notes that American leaders have drawn different lessons from the war. While some believe that Vietnam heralded the decline of American hegemony and the need for the United States to accommodate to changing circumstances, others think that Vietnam dramatized the need for an increase in American military strength to enable the United States to regain its hegemonic position. McCormick concludes that President Ronald Reagan and his advisers hoped to reassert the American role as the global policeman and to use the Strategic Defense Initiative to help the United States maintain its technological advantage in the international marketplace.

To recapitulate, the 1987 Sears Lecture series examines the Vietnam War from four different perspectives: a political leader, a professional soldier, a government consultant, and a university scholar. The speakers presented sharply contrasting views about the basic issues raised by the American experience in Vietnam. Did the United States send armed forces to Indochina in order to promote democratic institutions in South Vietnam or to protect Japanese economic interests and American strategic interests in Southeast Asia? Did the United States fail to accomplish its objectives in South Vietnam due to the behavior of irresponsible journalists and blundering politicians or because of the mistakes made by civilian analysts in the Pentagon and military officers directing the American war effort? Should the United States pursue a less ambitious foreign policy in the future or attempt to reassert its authority on a global basis? Although the speakers disagree among themselves over these fundamental questions, their arguments will help readers not only to gain a deeper understanding of the Vietnam War but also to participate with greater insight in the current debate about the role that the United States should play in world affairs.

# GEORGE S. MCGOVERN

George S. McGovern was born on 19 July 1922 in Avon, South Dakota. Serving as a pilot with the United States Army Air Force during World War II, he flew thirty-five bombing missions in Europe and won the Distinguished Flying Cross. McGovern received a B.A. in 1945 from Dakota Wesleyan University, and then he earned an M.A. and a Ph.D. in history from Northwestern University in 1949 and 1953. After serving as an assistant professor of history and political science at Dakota Wesleyan between 1949 and 1953, he decided to embark upon a political career. His first task as the executive secretary of the South Dakota Democratic Party from 1953 to 1955 was to help build a state-wide political organization. In 1956 he was elected to Congress and thereby became the first Democratic representative from South Dakota in twenty-two years. After a second term in the House, McGovern accepted an offer from President John F. Kennedy in 1961 to direct the Food for Peace Program. He was elected to the United States Senate in 1963 and served as Democratic senator from South Dakota for the next eighteen years.

An early opponent of American military intervention in Vietnam, McGovern became a major spokesman for antiwar congressmen. He delivered his first speech against American involvement in Vietnam in September 1963, when he called upon President Kennedy to withdraw American military advisers from Vietnam. McGovern argued that the Vietnam War was diverting resources from important domestic welfare programs in the United States while sacrificing the lives of many young Americans in a distant military adventure. He criticized the American government for supporting a dictatorial regime in South Vietnam and urged a return to peace through the process of negotiations. As he became increasingly concerned about American actions in Vietnam, McGovern decided to run for president on an antiwar platform. He won the Democratic nomination for president in 1972 and sought to make the war the major issue of the campaign. But McGovern suffered a landslide defeat at the hands of President Richard M. Nixon in the general election.

Besides lecturing on a wide variety of topics involving national and international affairs, McGovern has published numerous articles and books. His most important writings include *War Against Want: America's "Food for Peace Program,"* 1964; *A Time of War, a Time of Peace,* 1968; and *Grassroots: The Autobiography of George McGovern,* 1977. He has also contributed essays to *Atlantic, Saturday Review, Look, Commentary, New Republic,* and other periodicals.

# ONE

# AMERICA IN VIETNAM

## by Senator George S. McGovern

Some years ago, when Dr. Samuel Johnson was at the height of his literary powers, a rather bold young man brought a manuscript to him and asked Dr. Johnson if he would evaluate it. When he went back a couple of days later to get Dr. Johnson's opinion, the good doctor said: "Well, let me say that this manuscript is both good and original. The problem is that the good parts are not original and the original parts are not good." To avoid that danger here tonight, I am not going to speak from a manuscript but simply talk with you about my own perspective on one of the most controversial and tragic episodes in our entire national history. I believed then, twenty years ago, as I do now, that our involvement in the Vietnam War was the most painful political, moral, and military mistake in our entire history. Perhaps it was not as dangerous to us as the nuclear danger with which we still live or the relationship that we now have with the other superpower, the Soviet Union. But our involvement in the Vietnam War was a major tragedy.

When I use the word moral, or its opposite, immoral, in connection with this war, I am not talking about the motives of our policymakers, who doubtless were well-intentioned. Nor am I talking about the conduct of our troops, who did what they were asked to do by their superiors in Vietnam and the policymakers here at home and who fought bravely and courageously and sacrificed their own convenience generally, as forces have always done representing

the United States. At no time did I ever indict the motives of the
American soldiers who were involved in the fighting in Vietnam.
And one of the heartbreaking tragedies of this whole experience is
the difficulties these young men had in returning to a country that
was divided on the war issue. I, as one who long criticized our
involvement in Vietnam, have always felt a special obligation to try
to be understanding and sensitive about the difficulties these
young men faced once the war was over. When I came back from
World War II, like others coming back from that war, I was
treated in my home town as a hero. But not the young men who
were unfortunate enough to be called into the armed forces to participate in the Vietnam War.

For there was never a national consensus and never any
clear understanding in the Congress or elsewhere as to our fundamental purposes and objectives in the war, and the American
people were treated to a series of contradictions and disappointing
prophecies and inaccuracies about what was going on in Vietnam.
Looking back on the statements of very capable men, such as the
then secretary of state and the secretary of defense, Dean Rusk
and Robert McNamara, two of the most dedicated men who ever
served the United States government, the one consistent pattern in
their utterances is that they were virtually all wrong in terms of
the way history turned out in regard to the war in Vietnam.

Shortly after I left the United States Senate in January 1981,
I was invited by the University of New Orleans to offer a course on
the Vietnam War. In one of the discussions in that course, a student asked me if I thought there were lessons about our involvement in Vietnam that would help us determine what our course
should be in Nicaragua. Before I could answer the question, another student in the class said: "Well, I think if we want to know
what we ought to do in Nicaragua, it would be more important to
study the history of Nicaragua than to study the history of Vietnam." That may seem like a very obvious conclusion, but I
thought it was rather profound, and I think the same thing holds
true with respect to Vietnam.

If we wanted to understand the realities of Vietnam that
faced us when we made the decision to send our troops into combat there, it would have been a good idea to know something about
the history of Vietnam before we committed hundreds of thousands of young Americans who probably never would have heard
of Vietnam had it not been for our involvement. Professor John
Kenneth Galbraith has said that had we not become involved

there, Vietnam would have "continued in the obscurity which it so richly deserves." In any event, we did not give sufficient attention to the historical factors that were operating in Vietnam, and I think that, as much as anything, explains our mistaken policy toward that country.

In the 1960 presidential campaign between Richard Nixon and John F. Kennedy, at the end of the first debate on television, one of the reporters in the studio asked each candidate to describe in one minute what he regarded as his most important asset for the presidency. Mr. Nixon gave what I thought was a rather persuasive answer by saying that his experience doubtless was his greatest asset. Years of service in the House of Representatives and the Senate, eight years as vice president of the United States, and even more years as a world traveler. I wondered what Senator Kennedy, who was considerably less well known, would say. This is a rough summary of his response as I recall it: I believe that if I have any one quality that commends me to the presidency, it is my sense of history. By that I mean the capacity to understand the historical forces and traditions that have brought this country to a position of greatness and influence in the world; and beyond that, to understand the historical forces that are moving in our own time, those that we ought to identify with and those that we ought to oppose.

Well, as a former history teacher, I was sold on Kennedy's answer! I thought, here is a man that you can trust in the White House! Unfortunately, President Kennedy and his successors did not have sufficient historical knowledge of Vietnam required to make sound policy judgments.

Tonight I want to look at what I think were some of the historical realities that were not taken into proper account by our policymakers. This oversight explains why our intervention in Vietnam not only became a military disaster, in fact, the most striking defeat in our national history, but also why, more importantly, that policy needs to be viewed in retrospect as a political and diplomatic mistake of the greatest magnitude. We must realize that military policy ordinarily cannot be much more effective than the political and diplomatic underpinnings that give it focus and direction.

The associated states of Indochina—Vietnam, Laos, and Cambodia—were under the control of the French as colonies for about a century prior to the end of World War II. During that conflict, Indochina was overrun by Japan. In fact, one of the reasons the United States was on the verge of war with Japan was in reaction to Japan's move into Southeast Asia. So for some four years, with the French knocked out of the war in Europe, Japan presided over Vietnam and the rest of Southeast Asia.

But it was also during that period that Ho Chi Minh, then a rather young man who for many years had been working in the Vietnamese underground against the French, joined with the United States in the military effort against Japan. Some of my fellow pilots who were shot down over the Southeast Asian jungles in World War II found their way back to American lines with the cooperation and help of Ho Chi Minh and his guerrilla forces who were resisting the Japanese occupation of their country. During this period, Ho Chi Minh evidently believed that at the end of the war he could court the United States and achieve American support against what was expected to be a French effort to return and reestablish their colonies in Southeast Asia.

This was a view that seemed to be shared by the American president, Franklin D. Roosevelt, who wrote a memorandum late in World War II which said: "The French have milked that area for one hundred years. The people of Vietnam deserve something better." And what President Roosevelt had in mind was the establishment of a trusteeship under the United Nations that would govern the colonial peoples of Southeast Asia for a transitional period and prepare them for full independence. He certainly did not favor a return of French colonial rule in that part of the globe.

Unfortunately, Roosevelt died before World War II ended, and Harry S. Truman, who had very little knowledge of Southeast Asia, became president. Truman was a conscientious and dedicated public servant who did the best he could as president of the United States, but he nonetheless had very little understanding of what was going on in Southeast Asia. And the focus of American attention after World War II was not on Southeast Asia in any event, but rather it was on Europe and halting the perceived Soviet threat to Western Europe. The major American effort there was to build a Western alliance, including the French, that would provide a shield across Western Europe to stop what the Truman administration believed might be a Soviet probe into this crucial area against our historical allies. So after World War II, when messages started coming in from our foreign service people in the field in Indochina, and when Ho Chi Minh began asking for our help against the French, the Truman administration was more interested in cultivating the French than these little states in Southeast Asia.

American leaders were also concerned about the fact that Ho Chi Minh was a communist, and it was widely believed in the

United States that all communists took their orders from Moscow. Americans believed that Beijing also had extensive influence in Southeast Asian affairs, and that there was a great international network of communists, and that a communist anywhere in the world could be expected to behave pretty much on orders from Moscow or Beijing. So this double fear, the fear of losing French support in Western Europe for NATO and the fear of communism in Asia, sparked in part by Mao Zedong in China and Ho Chi Minh in Vietnam, was enough to get the Truman administration to reject any further overtures on the part of Ho Chi Minh. And presently we found ourselves involved in an eight-year effort to help the French reestablish their colonies in Southeast Asia against our own tradition of support for the self-determination of peoples. This policy ran counter to our own revolutionary heritage of rejecting outside control of this country by the British, and indeed, rejecting interference anywhere in this hemisphere by people from outside in violation of the Monroe Doctrine.

Nonetheless, we found ourselves from 1946 to 1954 supporting the French war effort in Indochina, eventually financing up to 75 or 80 percent of the French military cost. When the French met defeat in 1954 at the Battle of Dien Bien Phu, the then vice president of the United States, Richard Nixon, pleaded with President Eisenhower to send in American support—strategic support. If necessary, Nixon favored dropping nuclear bombs to save the failing French struggle against Ho Chi Minh at Dien Bien Phu. President Eisenhower, to his credit, replied: "I will not do this unless three conditions are met. In the first place, the French have to request it; secondly, the leaders of Congress (who were then Democrats, Sam Rayburn in the House, Lyndon Johnson in the Senate) have to agree with this; and thirdly, the British have to agree to go in with us." The first of these conditions was met. The French did request our help, but when our representatives talked to Winston Churchill and Anthony Eden about the British joining us, they turned thumbs down on the proposed military venture, saying, in effect, it was a no-win proposition. The two British leaders shared the view of many others who believed that it is impossible, at least at an acceptable cost, for Western forces to prevail in the jungles of Asia against an indigenous revolutionary army. Mr. Churchill in effect said: "We would be doing the Americans a great disfavor if we encouraged them in a foolish effort to become involved in a losing cause on behalf of the French." The same response came from leaders of Congress: Lyndon Johnson, Sam Rayburn, Hubert Humphrey, Mike Mansfield, and Richard Russell, the chairman of the Armed Services Committee. There was almost no support in the Congress for any kind of American military intervention. John Kennedy, as a member of the Senate, opposed it. And the French collapsed.

And then came the Geneva Conference* to end the fighting in Indochina. Ho Chi Minh agreed to call off the battle, which was decisively going his way, and go to the peace conference at Geneva. And there he agreed to a two-year armistice in preparation for an election to decide the future of Vietnam, North and South. And then came the second great American mistake (the first being to side with the French): instead of going along with an election that could have decided the future of Vietnam, we cast our lot with counterrevolutionary groups in South Vietnam that sought to resist the election process. President Eisenhower said at the time, and on the public record, that in a bona fide election in Vietnam, Ho Chi Minh would have won 80 percent or more of the vote both in the south and in the north. If that is true, and we believe in self-determination, what then was the rationalization for the policy that we pursued? Why did we set aside our support for the election called for in 1954 at Geneva and scheduled to take place two years later in July 1956? The rationalization, of course, was that we could not accept a communist regime in Vietnam—even one that might have been ratified by a popular election. Ho Chi Minh was the overwhelming choice of the rank and file both north and south.

It was a tragedy that almost breaks my heart to this day that an election was never held and instead we embarked upon a course of backing a succession of somewhat unpopular and ineffective governments in the south that were largely puppets of the United States. Puppets of the CIA, the State Department, and our military advisers. Ultimately failing even in that role, they had to be replaced by American forces that eventually comprised an army of 550,000 young men fighting in Vietnam for almost twenty years after that fateful decision to pass up the election agreed upon in 1954 at Geneva. And these American forces were to fight increasingly in a constantly losing and disappointing effort in Vietnam.

Meanwhile, the war was explained here by men such as Secretary of State Dean Rusk and President Johnson and later Presi-

---

*After the French defeat at Dien Bien Phu, an international conference was held in Geneva, Switzerland, between 8 May and 21 July 1954, to determine the political future of Indochina. The Geneva Accords imposed a cease-fire throughout Vietnam, provided for the temporary division of the country at the seventeenth parallel, and called for general elections two years later to achieve the peaceful reunification of Vietnam.

dent Nixon as a demonstration that we had learned the lessons of Munich. Whole generations of Americans, myself included, had grown up with the memory of the Munich Conference of 1938, when the allied powers, notably Britain and France, literally betrayed the integrity and survival of Czechoslovakia by granting Hitler's desire to take over a large chunk of what had been Czechoslovakia. And that pattern of feeding Hitler's appetite, historians still believe, and I think accurately, encouraged Hitler to go on to further conquests on the European continent. He had laid out in *Mein Kampf* and in public utterances his determination to take over a vast area in Europe and indeed to take over much of Western civilization. It was all there for anyone to read. He had built up the most powerful and aggressive military forces that existed anywhere in the world—in the air, on the land, and, to a certain extent, at sea. It was an unrivaled military machine with the most aggressive kind of announced policy. And doubtless it was right to conclude, as many people did at the time, myself included, that it was a mistake to feed the appetite of a monster like Adolf Hitler by giving up half of Czechoslovakia, which was ready and willing to fight for its independence and survival with any help or encouragement from its Western backers and allies.

But that European lesson was misapplied in Vietnam, where Ho Chi Minh was portrayed as the new Hitler. It is true that Ho Chi Minh was no saint. He was an admitted communist. He was a tough, hard-boiled, and in some respects, ruthless leader. But he was an indigenous Vietnamese nationalist who had, if not the affection, the respect and support of most of the people in both halves of Vietnam. Yet the Vietnamese conflict was always described both by the Johnson administration and the Nixon administration as aggression from the north against the south and therefore similar to Hitler's aggression against Czechoslovakia. But the reality is that it was essentially a struggle between two groups of Vietnamese for control of their country: one group that had fought against the French and tried to establish independence; another group which to a great extent had played little or no role in that anticolonial struggle or, in some cases, had gone along without protest against French rule.

In any event, the conflict in Vietnam against the government that we helped install in Saigon under President Diem was initiated in the south with communist cadres participating but also with broad support across the countryside. And this is why the more American arms that flowed into the South Vietnamese army that we were backing, the more those arms found their way into the hands of the guerrilla forces that had better connections at the grass roots. We were the supply sergeant for both the South Vietnamese government, which we were officially backing, and the Vietcong, which we regarded as the enemy. The weapons on both sides came from the United States.

It was very difficult during the war in Vietnam even to identify who was a friend and who was a foe. This was one of the things that frustrated our forces. I recall one time visiting Vietnam during the war when my son-in-law was fighting with the 3rd Marines. I spent part of the Thanksgiving period with him in November 1965, early in the war. During my visit, I had an opportunity to talk with a general who was in charge of our air operations in a crucial part of Vietnam. He told me about his houseboy, as he called him, a young Vietnamese man who was working for him at his house taking care of the domestic chores. This young man had begun asking him if he could take off the weekends to visit his brother. After this happened three or four times, the general asked: "Where does your brother live and what does he do?" The young man replied: "He's a captain with the Vietcong." This was the nature of the war. It was very difficult to know where to draw the line between friend and foe.

My son-in-law lives with the haunting memory of being out on patrol one day when he heard a rustle in the brush ahead and turned and fired almost instinctively only to discover just as he was squeezing the trigger that he was shooting a little girl seven or eight years old. He killed her accidentally thinking she was an enemy. And she could have been the enemy. Even the children set booby traps and threw grenades and participated in the struggle. It was a very difficult and frustrating operation for American forces to fight under those conditions. And in our frustration, we increasingly used sophisticated heavy American firepower in an attempt to kill the Vietcong guerrillas but discovered that we were killing more innocent people than enemy soldiers.

We went to Vietnam not to add to the misery of the people, but by the time we left we had dropped more bombs on this tiny strip of territory in the jungles of Southeast Asia than were dropped on the continents of Asia, Africa, and Europe during the Second World War, when I did my share of dropping bombs and seeing the destructive character of war. But at least then we were trying to hit highly industrialized targets or military concentrations. In Vietnam, in the effort to do what we thought was winning the hearts and minds of people to the cause of freedom, we were turning the people of the country against us and against the

American-sponsored government in Saigon by blowing up their villages and burning their homes. We rooted out the infrastructure of the Vietcong through the Phoenix Program, which was an American-led effort to assassinate village leaders and teachers and lawyers and doctors who might be sympathetic to the Vietcong cause, and used highly dangerous chemicals to kill the foliage so that we could expose the Vietcong forces to the aerial view of helicopters and bombers and also starve out people in certain selected areas. All of these things came to haunt American forces who were in Vietnam and to trouble the conscience of Americans back home who were asked to support this carnage and killing and destruction of people in the name of freedom and in the name of human dignity. However good the motives of the people who took us into this enterprise may have been, they did not count the realities that we were going to confront in Southeast Asia, and as a consequence the policy came to naught.

There was another reason the United States was fighting in Vietnam in addition to checking communism in the personage of Ho Chi Minh and the Vietcong, and that is the fear of falling dominoes. All here, I am sure, from the youngest to the oldest, have heard of the domino theory under which it was said by American policymakers, first by President Eisenhower and then by his successors, that countries were like dominoes, that if one of them fell to the communists, the spillover would take down the one next door. According to this theory, if Vietnam went to the communists, Thailand would follow, then would come the Philippines, Indonesia, Australia, Japan, and finally, Hawaii and San Francisco. I know we laugh about this now, but that was the theory. One of the Vietnam vets, home on leave in my state during the time that I was criticizing our involvement in Vietnam, attacked me. He said: "George McGovern doesn't understand that if we don't stop the communists in Vietnam, we're going to have to fight them on the streets of Aberdeen, South Dakota." People believed that, I am embarrassed to say. We were left to wonder how the Vietnamese, even with the help of Chinese junks, would get by the Seventh Fleet on their way to San Francisco, but I suppose it would happen the same way that the Sandinistas would get to Texas, which so worries President Reagan.

I am amazed at how slowly people learn history when, after all the tragic experience with Vietnam, the president of the United States can seriously tell the people of this country that we are helping the Contras because we do not want the Sandinistas in Texas, which is only hours away from Nicaragua by car. These Sandinistas cannot even seem to get together in the same car, let alone reach Texas. But nonetheless, that was the argument in Vietnam—that we had to stand against the communists in Vietnam, or we would be facing them in some more crucial country next year.

The argument behind all this, again, was based on the assumption that Ho Chi Minh was simply a puppet of Beijing, and to a lesser extent, of Moscow. Anyone who has studied the history of Vietnam would know that if there is any one country in the world that the Vietnamese hate above all others it is China. And it does not make any difference whether the Vietnamese are under communist rule or the mandate of heaven, or whatever. There has never been any love lost between China and Vietnam. At one point, when Ho Chi Minh was maneuvering very early in 1946 to get Chinese troops out of Vietnam, he made a deal with the French, and one of his communist colleagues attacked him for doing something that seemed to be playing into the hands of the Western world. Ho Chi Minh responded with a very colorful phrase. He said: "I would rather smell French dung for five years than eat Chinese dung for a thousand years." And this was the way the Vietnamese felt, and lo and behold, once the United States got out of Vietnam, the next war in Southeast Asia was between Vietnam and China. These two countries could hardly wait to get at each other once they no longer had the Americans to unite them, and I suspect that one of the bizarre by-products of the Vietnam War is that it did as much as anything in that whole period to keep the communist leaders in Moscow and Beijing and Hanoi at least talking to each other.

And the war did another thing—it diverted much of the energy and the intelligence and the time and the resources of the United States government to a little country in Southeast Asia where we scarcely had any national interest. That absorbed so much of our interest that we missed great opportunities to make steady improvement in regard to other foreign policy and national security problems of infinitely greater importance to the well-being of the United States, such as the Middle East and Soviet-American relations, which were beginning to improve in the early 1960s first under President Eisenhower and then under President Kennedy. And one of the things that soured the beginning of a better relationship between the two superpowers, which has been the most crucial foreign policy problem since World War II, was the fact that the United States and the Soviet Union were divided over the issue of Vietnam. It was not so much that the Soviets were all that dedicated to a Ho Chi Minh victory, but simply that here was a communist government, a communist colleague, and they felt obligated to maintain some kind of relationship with Hanoi by supplying arms and giving encouragement to the North Vietnamese.

Vietnam, I think it is safe to say, for two years absorbed the principal energies and imagination and diplomatic skills and, I might add, economic resources of the United States. It is no accident that chronic inflation in this country began in 1965 with the decision to escalate the war in Vietnam in a major way without any of the usual restraints. We had no price controls as we had always had in previous wars, no rationing, no increase in taxes, no excess profits tax on war manufacturers, nothing of that kind. It was business as usual here at home. The Great Society program was torpedoed by the rising cost of the war and the inflation that it brought. The Vietnam War brought about the eclipse of the great society that President Johnson dreamed of building in the United States. He was a good president in terms of his vision for this country: quality education, civil justice, decent housing, and strong agricultural programs. Those things that he really knew and understood were diminished by the grinding impact of this war on the American economy and on American society.

The Vietnam War divided and confused the people of the United States as nothing else has since the Civil War of the 1860s. This is where the "credibility gap" was born in American politics—the difference between the realities of Vietnam and what leaders were telling us. We were told, for example, that the principal problem in achieving victory in Vietnam was the dissenters within American society. The policymakers in Washington were so anxious to sell that line that they were willing to attempt to intimidate and silence free speech in the United States. In other words, they exhibited a willingness to invest so much blood and treasure in supposedly advancing freedom to the Vietnamese that they would sacrifice liberty here at home by calling for an end to dissent and criticism—the very lifeblood of a healthy democracy. So there were descriptions of the war critics as "nervous Nellies," as they were one time called by the president, warnings that we were not going to put our tail between our legs and sneak out of Vietnam like a whipped dog, and boasts that we were going to nail that coonskin to the wall. All kinds of language like that emanated from the White House. "I'm not going to be the first president to lose an American war," Lyndon Johnson insisted. "I'm not going to sit in a rocking chair and let freedom go down the drain."

All this brave talk, which the American people eventually saw through, was a mask for a failing and an impossible policy in

Vietnam. Finally President Johnson, who in 1964 had scored one of the greatest landslide victories in American history, was forced to leave the White House and not seek reelection in 1968. The Vietnam War divided the Democratic party especially. Somehow the Republicans were always able to finesse the war issue better than the Democrats. There was not much debate about it inside the Republican party. There were a great many Republicans disturbed about what the United States was doing in Vietnam, but their candidates took the view that the war was the president's responsibility and they were not going to second-guess him. The Democrats had their fights right out in the open with Robert Kennedy and Eugene McCarthy challenging Johnson for the presidential nomination in 1968 and others of us cheering them on.

Then came 1972 and my own candidacy, which was based more than anything else on the anguish that I felt over our mistaken policy in Vietnam. My concern began out of intellectual curiosity, and then it deepened into genuine alarm and concern about what we were doing, supposedly in the name of freedom. And finally, Vietnam became an obsession with me that I could not get out of my being. I carried the war in my stomach and heart and mind for ten years above any other concern in public life. And this is what set the stage for me to run for the presidency in 1972. As a junior senator from a little state like South Dakota, I was nominated for president because I struck a chord with a part of the American public who wanted the war brought to an end. I think President Nixon sensed that, and he very shrewdly talked about ending the war with honor—peace with honor. The implication was that I would end it with dishonor. My view was that, if I were president of the United States, I would withdraw American forces from Vietnam within sixty days subject only, of course, to the release of our prisoners as the withdrawal took place. President Nixon orchestrated the notion that we were staying in Vietnam to get the prisoners out, notwithstanding the fact that the longer we stayed, the more American prisoners were captured. They were captured largely in bombing raids, and prisoners ordinarily do not get out of wars until they are over. There was not anything unusual about prisoners being held in Vietnam until the war ended.

In any event, that kind of rhetoric from the beginning masked the follies of the war, but it did not, I suggest to you, mislead millions of Americans who gathered in demonstrations, who wrote letters, who came to Washington, who conducted meetings in their churches, who held teach-ins in their classrooms, and who participated in the street marches. You almost had to live through all of those things to realize how inflamed this country was over the issue of Vietnam.

I was at Kent State University the other night, where four students were shot down by the Ohio National Guard in one of the demonstrations on that campus. A couple of those students just happened to be walking across the campus between classes when they were hit by bullets. This tragedy was symbolic of the way the Vietnam War had poisoned internal dialogue and discussion in the United States. And so in the end we failed, and the credibility gap came into being. I am not going to belabor this point tonight, but let me just suggest that the whole Watergate episode★ had its origins in the Vietnam War. It grew out of the conspiratorial atmosphere, the credibility problems, and the manipulative character of our leaders during the war. President Nixon, as many of you might know, was secretly bombing Cambodia, a neutral country, while publically denying it to the Congress of the United States and to the American public. This went on for fourteen months—young pilots being asked to forge the records of bombing missions, senior officers being asked to fake those records. These serious violations of federal law were required by the commander-in-chief of the armed forces who ordered the attacks against a neutral country that was trying its best to avoid involvement in the Vietnam conflict. The bombing in Cambodia contributed to the collapse of the Sihanouk government. And Prince Norodom Sihanouk was eventually replaced by a crazy man, Pol Pot, a Cambodian communist who went on a killing campaign that eventually slaughtered two million Cambodian citizens. This was, perhaps, the greatest single cost of our involvement in Indochina. The killing in Cambodia was not done by the Vietnamese who were supposed to be the domino threat next door; it was done by Cambodians who came to power against their own people, I think in part because of the immoral and illegal secret bombing that did such damage to the infrastructure of Cambodia. This was one of the more tragic by-products of our military involvement in Indochina.

In the end, the policy failed. I want to close on these two notes because I think they capture, in a sense, some of the lessons

---

★On 22 June 1972, several men were caught burglarizing the Democratic Party National Headquarters at the Watergate office complex in Washington, D.C. Evidence gradually mounted that President Richard M. Nixon had tried to cover up their effort to help assure his reelection. Eventually the House Judiciary Committee charged Nixon with obstructing justice and abusing his power, and the Supreme Court ordered him to turn over key tapes dealing with the Watergate scandal. On 9 August 1974, Nixon resigned the presidency in order to avoid the humiliation of impeachment.

of the Vietnam War. In the first place, as I have said, even a policy that turns out to be immoral need not lead us to the conclusion that the motives of the policymakers who established that policy were immoral. They were guilty, I think, of what Thackeray described as "the mischief which the very virtuous do." Although they supposedly acted to advance freedom, they accomplished the mischief of people who did not know what they were doing despite whatever virtue they had. And secondly I end with a warning which I would like to leave with you from the British conservative of the last century, Edmund Burke, who warned the people of that time against rash actions. "A conscientious man," he declared, "will be cautious how he deals in blood." I hope we remember that warning when we are looking at Nicaragua and other parts of the globe in the years to come.

---

QUESTION: Since Lyndon Johnson, while serving as a senator, opposed our involvement or getting involved in Vietnam, why did he after becoming president make such a gigantic escalation in 1965? Did he believe some of his own propaganda that he used to get Congress to approve the Gulf of Tonkin Resolution?

ANSWER: Well, that is a good question. You can make the question even more complicated by remembering the 1964 presidential campaign that Johnson won over Barry Goldwater by an enormous margin, about the same margin as Nixon won over me, or Reagan won over Mondale. By the way, it is hazardous to give people that big an election win. You especially do not want to let a California politician win an election by a margin of forty-nine to one! In any event, Johnson said in his 1964 campaign: "We're not going north, we're not going south. We're not going to send American boys to fight battles that have to be won by Asian boys." The Democratic presidential cry of 1964 was: "We seek no wider war." I was out campaigning for Johnson, warning people that if Goldwater were elected, we would expand the war. We would start bombing, we would send in American troops; but with Lyndon Johnson as our president, we would have "no wider war." I believed that. And that was his history on this issue.

I think what happened is that Johnson took over the White House with no warning after the assassination of John Kennedy. He kept the same team that had advised Kennedy: Dean Rusk at the State Department, Robert McNamara at the Defense Department, McGeorge Bundy and Walt Rostow in the national security apparatus at the White House, and all the others. And when the war in Vietnam started to turn badly, Johnson had to make a decision. Kennedy had never been forced to decide what he would do if the Vietcong started to win because the war was still inconclusive at that point. But when our advisers out in the field, our senior military men in Vietnam, started telling Johnson that the Saigon government would fall if we did not send in American forces, he began to fear that the highly popular president from Massachusetts, John Kennedy, who went to his death in a blaze of glory at the height of his power and vitality—that he would be replaced by the first president to preside over an American defeat. I think it was very difficult for a man raised in the shadow of the Alamo to give up under that kind of pressure.

I talked to Johnson privately before I publically criticized his policy. It was very difficult for me as a young Democratic senator to publically criticize my own Democratic president. In fact, it was not easy with any of the presidents, Republican or Democrat. None of us like to criticize the commander-in-chief, particularly when we have forces in battle. So I talked privately with him about these things, about my concerns. And what I saw was the painful recognition on his part that he might look like a loser, a weakling. And furthermore, Johnson was told by his advisers that the credibility of the United States was on the line. If our allies cannot depend on us in Vietnam, how can they depend on us in the Middle East? If they could not depend on us in Vietnam, why would our allies in Western Europe assume that we would go to their help? Now these arguments were made, notwithstanding the fact that none of our allies supported what we were doing in Vietnam. They all wanted us to get the hell out of there.

Johnson, like both his predecessors and his successors, did not want to face the painful reality that the United States could not prevail militarily in Vietnam at an acceptable cost. Now I think everybody knows that if we had decided to go for an all-out military victory, we could have pulvarized every living thing in Indochina with a few nuclear weapons. But we did not go there to kill people. We went there to make life better for people and advance the cause of freedom and security, so that ruled out the possibility of using nuclear weapons. It also cast into serious question the massive bombardment we made with conventional weapons and with napalm and other things. But Johnson seemed to believe his advisers—one more shot and we can turn it around.

I am positive, after the talks I had with him, that Johnson never intended on sending a half million soldiers into Vietnam. I do not think he ever envisioned that; but when fifty thousand could not do the job, then it became seventy-five thousand; and when they could not do the job, it was a hundred and a quarter thousand. Then it got up to two hundred thousand, and it just kept going up. I am sure that all through this, Johnson saw himself as the man of restraint who was saying "no, no" to the people who wanted more bombing, who wanted more troops. He saw himself, not as a wild imperialist, but as a cautious, shrewd Texas politician. He was not going to let people rush him into a policy of escalation, but over the course of time, the United States ended up with five hundred and fifty thousand troops in Vietnam, and the last word from General Westmoreland was that he could not prevail without another two hundred and fifty thousand men. And that was when Clark Clifford, the secretary of defense, became a dove and broke with Lyndon Johnson.

QUESTION: Because of the Vietnam experience, you and others passed the War Powers Act* and other legislation to reduce the authority of the president and to restore checks and balances in the government. Now, in light of the recent misadventures of the National Security Council with respect to selling arms to Iran and aiding the Contras, do you think that that legislation ought to be revised and if so, in which direction?

ANSWER: Yes. I think that the War Powers Act should be revised. I do not think that it has enough teeth in it. It was a good idea and I supported it, although I must say two or three of the senators who were better lawyers than I am (I am not a lawyer at all) saw some of the loopholes in that law from the beginning. Thomas Eagleton of Missouri voted against the War Powers Act, not because he did not want to limit the powers of the president, but because he thought the measure would give the impression of doing that without really having the teeth to do so. And in that sense, the War Powers Act might be even weaker than what we already had: the Constitution of the United States saying that the power to declare war resides in the Congress. If our presidents would just heed the Constitution, we could get by without the War Powers Act.

I think most of the troubles we have gotten into since World War II, whether under Truman, Kennedy, Johnson, Nixon,

---

*On 7 November 1973, Congress overrode a veto by President Richard M. Nixon and passed the War Powers Act. The measure required that in the future the president must report to Congress within forty-eight hours if he committed American military forces overseas and withdraw them within sixty days unless Congress approved the action.

Reagan, or whoever happened to be in the White House (it does not seem to make much difference whether they were Republicans or Democrats) has been when presidents broke the Constitution and did some screwball, secretive thing that was illegal, on the grounds that we had to do it to keep up with the Russians. Well, the United States does not have to copy every trick and dirty gimmick that the Russians dream up in order to be a strong country. And I think that the more we violate our Constitution, the more we get into problems that really do not serve our national security. You know, it is against the law to sell arms to Iran. It is against the intent of the law when Congress passes a law to prevent aid going to the Contras, for the president to go on television and urge people to find some way to circumvent the Congress.

It is not surprising to me that Lieutenant Colonel Oliver North picked up the message. It would be ridiculous to argue that this lieutenant colonel, who after all is trained to follow orders and who, I am told, is a disciplined officer, is to blame for all of these machinations. North was carrying out what he believed to be the intended policy of the United States government. But I wish he would quit pleading the fifth amendment and tell the truth about what actually went on. If we really want to know what the truth is, the president ought to call North into his office and ask him what he was doing.

In any event, the point of this is yes, strengthen the War Powers Act. But we probably would not need it if presidents would just heed the Constitution of the United States which puts the power to declare war in the hands of Congress. And Congress ought to wake up to this fact.

QUESTION: Given the fact that we were supposedly in Vietnam to support the cause of freedom and democracy, why would we consequently install military dictatorships in some countries or regimes that actually repress the people even more than the supposedly communist governments that would have been there naturally?

ANSWER: Well, I think that your question states the situation in the way that it is posed. We really have not been consistent on the commitment to support governments that practice freedom. We have backed scoundrels all over the world since World War II, as long as they did what we wanted them to do while waving an anticommunist banner. Look how long we stayed with Ferdinand Marcos in the Philippines. I want to say that it is to the credit of President Reagan that he finally faced a reality there. How much he personally is responsible for that, I do not know. In any event, it was on his watch, as he puts it, when we got rid of Marcos. But the question is: why did we back Marcos all these years when we knew he was ripping off the country and violating all kinds of our own provisions with regard to the assistance we were giving him? Why did we go along with so many military dictators simply because they were waving an anticommunist banner? I think that is the real reason why the Reagan Administration is backing the Contras. It is not so much that the White House yearns for more press freedom in Nicaragua. I do not think our leaders are being entirely candid when they say that we are in Nicaragua to enlarge the writ of human freedom. The Contras have not been noted for their devotion to freedom. They are more interested in drug running and getting back into power to carry out the mischief they did under Somoza* than they are in advancing the cause of freedom. By the way, our historical relationship to Nicaragua has been anything but a consistent testament to our interest in freedom, going back almost a hundred years.

QUESTION: I would like your opinion on the theory that our ten-year involvement in Vietnam gave other countries in Southeast Asia time to strengthen their own national governments to protect them from possible destabilization later.

ANSWER: Well, that is an interesting question. Did our willingness to stand in Vietnam for ten years permit some of the governments in the area to develop indigenous institutions to govern themselves? My answer would be no, that was not one of the by-products of it. I think countries stand or fall largely on the basis of the commitment they bring themselves to independence and to freedom. And I do not think that what we were doing in Vietnam necessarily resulted in Indonesia turning against the communists. I cite, as one example, that the American ambassador in Indonesia, when asked if it were true that the people in that country turned against the communists because they saw the United States standing against communism in Vietnam, replied: "Well, only in the sense that we were so busily involved in Vietnam that we didn't have time to intervene in Indonesia and screw it up for

---

*The Somoza family dynasty in Nicaragua received strong support from the United States. After assuming power in Managua in 1936, Anastasio Somoza used the National Guard to maintain control over the Nicaraguan people. The dictator died in 1956, but his two sons continued to rule the country. Anastasio, Jr., became president in 1966, but he fled from Nicaragua in 1979 when the Sandinista rebels seized power.

them." Now that statement comes from a thoughtful, rather conservative American ambassador. I do not think that what we did in Vietnam contributed very much for good or ill to the neighboring countries with the exception of poor Cambodia, which got caught in the vise, and Laos. But the rest of the countries in Southeast Asia, I think, have developed pretty much as they would have had we never been involved in Vietnam. I do not see any evidence to the contrary.

QUESTION: It took an inordinate amount of time to rally the American people against the Vietnam War. Do you feel that that could be related to the incredibly long time that it has taken to rally public sentiment against the nuclear madness that the United States has perpetrated?

ANSWER: Well, it does take time to change American public opinion in the face of steadfast assurances from our top officials that the policy that we are pursuing is the right one. This is particularly true when the policy has the kind of broad, bipartisan support in the top leadership of the United States that our Vietnam policy had. It was not simply that Lyndon Johnson or Richard Nixon backed our course in Vietnam. It was the fact that the top leadership in both political parties was pretty well united behind that policy. So it does take time for dissonant elements to make their case, particularly when the president has the capacity to go on prime-time television and explain, over a period of fifteen minutes or a half hour, why the policy is good. That has a greater impact on many people than what they perceive as a bunch of disturbed, somewhat hysterical protestors out in the street yelling against the government. I am exaggerating, but that is the way it came across to a great many people.

Those people out in the streets were my supporters, but in many cases they made tactical errors that hurt the antiwar cause. Sometimes they were too strident. Maybe there were times when I was too strident. The American people do not want to be told that a policy of the United States government is immoral, or foolish, or stupid. Maybe you should not use words like that when you are trying to persuade people who are on the fence to come over to your side. So it is quite possible that some of us in the antiwar movement were a little too strident in the way we approached others. I tried not to be.

I wanted to work through an orderly and restrained process, and so I ran for the presidency and attempted the traditional ways of changing opinion in this country. I thought we should give the political process a test and see if we could bring about change in that way rather than by encouraging people to barricade themselves in the dean's office, stop traffic in the street, or use similar tactics that might irritate a lot of people who were not, perhaps, as understanding of the antiwar feeling as we wished they would have been. But I think for all of those reasons the antiwar effort was slowed.

I was puzzled, frankly, after all of the recent revelations about the Iran-Contra fiasco, that the House voted to continue the aid for the rebels in Nicaragua. I thought the House would stand up against such aid this time, and I was quite surprised about the outcome of the vote. Now we have a filibuster in the Senate to prevent a vote on the issue. But I am still hopeful that maybe we will be a little quicker to react than we were in regard to Vietnam if there is a move toward deeper American involvement in Nicaragua. We really have no business being militarily active there.

QUESTION: Sir, this might sound like an embarrassing question, but I wanted to ask you: What mistakes do you feel you made in the campaign of 1972? Why were you not able to defeat a president who lied to the American people, whose policies flouted international law and American law, and lead as you know to gross violations of human rights?

ANSWER: Well, I keep asking myself that question. There undoubtedly were mistakes in the campaign of 1972 made on my part and others, but I can tell you that I think we were right on all of the essential points that we were trying to get across to the American public. I thought we were right then, and I still do today, fifteen years later. Essentially, what the McGovern campaign wanted was simply for this country to live up to its historical values. We had a slogan: "Come Home America." It was not a plea for isolationism; it was a plea for America to return to the constitutional and ethical and political ideals that had given birth to us as a country. We wanted a return to the ideals of Thomas Jefferson and Abraham Lincoln and James Madison and all the others who spelled out in some of the most inspired language what a great country like the United States ought to stand for. And that was what we were trying to do. But I realize that we made some mistakes. I suppose the most costly one was over the vice-presidential selection that came so quickly after I was nominated. The American people really did not know an awful lot about me, and all of a sudden I was nominated by the Democrats for the presidency. The first thing one does as the nominee is to pick a running mate, and so that is the first opportunity for the people around the country to evaluate the judgment of the presidential candidate. Well, unwittingly, I picked a man with a fifteen-year history of mental illness. Maybe I should have known about his problem. I did not. I did not even know much about mental illness, to tell you the truth, or whether that was a barrier, nor did I know how to handle it once the news broke in the press. I thought I had picked a man who was a very good senator. I still think he was an excellent senator and might have been a very good president, but that was not what most of the psychiatrists were telling me. So that was very costly, and I, of course, deeply regret that error. But I am not sure that I should carry the full blame. One likes to think that in a situation like that others would also be involved with some sense of responsibility.

QUESTION: This is actually a two-part question. First off, what are your feelings concerning the present POW-MIA situation? And secondly, what is the stance of the Vietnamese government on this issue?

ANSWER: It is my own view that there are no American POWs in Vietnam. I know that the families of the missing people and the people who were taken as prisoners hope that they are still alive, but I think the evidence is overwhelming that there are none. There will continue to be rumors and people swearing they saw one walking across the street, or they know somebody that saw one. But my view, as one who has looked into this matter very carefully, and I have been to Vietnam a number of times, is that there are no surviving American prisoners of war.

In every war there are many listed as "missing in action." My own navigator is still missing in action from World War II. I have no idea what happened to him. He was flying with another crew the day his plane was hit, and he was seen bailing out, but nobody knows what happened to him. He was never captured, at least there was no record of it; perhaps he was shot while dropping, shot in his parachute by civilians. But nobody knows. He is still listed as missing in action. And, in Europe where we fought on more or less level terrain, we were less likely to have soldiers missing in action than in the jungles of Vietnam.

I think it is amazing that we had so few men missing in action in Vietnam. The army and the military forces did a marvelous job getting people back to American lines and getting all the prisoners out of Vietnam and searching for MIAs. I think that everything humanly possible has been done. We have a congressman who has become a specialist on this subject—Sonny Montgomery in Mississippi—and he would be proud for me to say that there is no bigger hawk in Congress than Sonny Montgomery. He supported the Vietnam War right up until the American ambassador was lifted off the roof of his residence in Saigon. He still thinks it was right for the United States to have fought the communists in Vietnam. So Sonny Montgomery took a special interest in this question, and he headed a subcommittee in the House that for several years tried to find evidence of POWs and MIAs in Vietnam. He went there many times with his committee, accompanied by professional Senate and House investigators, but he finally concluded after years of searching that there were none.

One would have to concede that there may be some shell-shocked victim of the war living in a jungle village after having been adopted by the natives or something like that. But if you stop to think about it, the Vietnamese government would have no selfish interest in holding American prisoners of war or hiding anyone missing in action. They never had any interest in holding prisoners one day beyond the end of the war. I think the evidence is overwhelming that this issue grows out of the understandable anguish of the survivors in the United States, who want somehow to believe that their son or husband or brother is still alive. And that if we would just work a little harder, somehow they would come home. This is understandable, and the slightest rumor will set off a new move to locate Americans thought to be missing in Vietnam. But I would be willing to stake my own public judgment on the fact that this is a blind alley. The Vietnamese, in spite of the fact that we refuse to recognize them, trade with them, or have anything to do with them, have worked very hard, I think it is fair to say, to find any Americans still listed as missing in action. When they have found bodies, they have sent the remains back to the United States.

I personally went to Vietnam because I thought, as a critic of the war, I should be especially diligent in responding to soldiers who may have been wounded or missing or taken prisoner. So I spent considerable time in Vietnam and talked to Pham Van Dong, who was then the premier of the country after the death of Ho Chi Minh. He said: "Well, Senator, you have to understand that we have some missing in action, too." And, of course, they run hundreds of times the size of our losses. We had fifty-eight thousand people killed in Vietnam, which is tragic; but they lost probably two million people in the war, and they do not have the technical resources that we do to identify remains. They have been conducting a search for their missing, and, I think under the circumstances, they have actually done rather well in trying to cooperate with us on this issue. I think they are doing it out of self-interest because they hope that some day we will see fit to recognize them as a nation and carry on trade and diplomacy with them just as we do with other communist countries—even the big ones, Russia and China. We have got a hang-up concerning small communist countries. We are scared to death of the Cubans or the Nicaraguans or the North Koreans or the Angolans. Little impoverished countries. Once these tiny states become Marxist, we tremble in our shoes. We will not even permit an embassy. It is all right to have relations with Russia or with China. If you want to be popular on the cocktail circuit, just go to China now and come back and tell how wonderful it is: "Great progress they're making in China. Fascinating country, you know; and there's just a billion communists there—there's really nothing to worry about, but just watch out for those Vietnamese!"

# WILLIAM C. WESTMORELAND

**W**illiam C. Westmoreland was born on 26 March 1914 in Spartanburg County, South Carolina. He entered the United States Military Academy in 1932 and graduated in 1936 as first captain (the senior cadet in the corps). After completing his military education at West Point, Westmoreland embarked upon a long and distinguished career in the United States Army. During World War II, he served in North Africa, Sicily, France, and Germany. Westmoreland became the chief of staff of the 9th Infantry Division in 1944, the chief of staff of the 82nd Airborne Division in 1947, and an instructor at the Army War College in Fort Levenworth in 1951. During the Korean War, he commanded the 187th Airborne Infantry Regimental Combat Team. After attending the Advanced Management Program at Harvard University in 1954, he served as the secretary of the Army General Staff from 1955 to 1958, the commander of the 101st Airborne Division from 1958 to 1960, and the superintendent of the United States Military Academy from 1960 to 1963.

Following his stint at West Point, Westmoreland served as the commander of the United States Military Assistance Command, Vietnam (MACV) between 1964 and 1968. He first sought a holding action combined with spoiling attacks to prevent a major enemy offensive while the United States constructed a huge logistical infrastructure to support a larger combat force in South Vietnam. As the American troop strength increased, Westmoreland turned to a strategy of attrition. He sent American and South Vietnamese forces on search and destroy missions in an effort to kill, wound, or capture enemy troops faster than they could be resupplied through recruitment in South Vietnam or infiltration from North Vietnam. But the American people became increasingly impatient with the Vietnam War as they found themselves paying an escalating price both in terms of blood and treasure, and after the communist offensive during the Tet celebration in 1968, President Lyndon B. Johnson decided to replace Westmoreland as the MACV commander in Saigon. Following his return home, Westmoreland served as the chief of staff of the United States Army until 1972, when he retired from active duty.

Westmoreland is a highly decorated soldier. He received more than thirty awards for military service, including the Legion of Merit, the Bronze Star, and the Air Medal. He was also named "Man of the Year" in 1965 by *Time* magazine.

Westmoreland kept a journal of his years in Vietnam, and in 1976 he used much of this material for his book entitled *A Soldier Reports*. He has also written numerous articles in newspapers and magazines about the American war effort in Vietnam.

Westmoreland came back into the headlines in 1982 when the CBS News documentary "The Uncounted Enemy: A Vietnam Deception" accused him of manipulating data on enemy troop strength in 1967 to indicate that the United States was making great military progress in South Vietnam. Westmoreland responded by filing a libel suit against CBS, but the issue was settled out of court in 1985 without any payments by either party.

# TWO

# VIETNAM IN PERSPECTIVE

## by General William C. Westmoreland

You know, every human endeavor has its pundits, its alleged experts, its philosophers, or its arm-chair quarterbacks. And military endeavors are no exception. Therefore I will begin my talk by quoting several recognized military philosophers or practitioners who have suggested certain parameters associated with the prosecution of war. The first known and respected writer on military strategy and tactics, who wrote five hundred years before Christ, was a Chinese man by the name of Sun Tzu.* He wrote profoundly, and among other things he said: "There has never been a protracted war from which a country has benefited." And the Duke of Wellington, the victor over Napoleon at Waterloo, told the House of Lords: "A great country cannot wage a little war." The Vietnam War was summarized by the distinguished diplomat Ellsworth Bunker, who was our ambassador in Saigon for five years and a remarkable man. He described the Vietnam War as a limited war with a limited objective with limited public support, and I add "with limited results."

These quotes set the stage for my talk tonight, in which I will explore the complexities and frustrations of the war in Viet-

---

*Sun Tzu, a Chinese strategic thinker, wrote the earliest known treatises on warfare. He attempted to formulate a rational basis for the conduct of military operations. His essays on "The Art of War," composed during the fourth century B.C., have had a profound influence on Oriental military thought.

nam. As a useful, simplistic outline for my talk, I refer to the cele-
brated Karl von Clausewitz,* generally accepted as the most
profound writer on military strategy, who has suggested that war,
to be successful, must be based on three criteria. First, there must
be a clear objective backed by a practical strategy. Second, the war
must be prosecuted by appropriate operational instruments. And
finally, a war, to be successful, must be backed by the passions of
the people of the nation. Now first let me discuss the need for a
clear objective backed by a practical strategy.

The objective of the United States government in Vietnam
was made clear by the Truman Doctrine of 1947. The Truman
Doctrine came after World War II had been concluded, the fighting had stopped, and international arrangements were in disarray.
It became very clear that the Soviet Union was going to grab as
much real estate as possible in the aftermath of that great war.
Thus, the Truman Doctrine said in essence: "We will not allow a
little country to be pushed around and be taken over by the communists. Somebody has to come to their rescue and we will do
that." Next, we had the Eisenhower strategy of containment, and
then President Kennedy's inaugural words, which I will refer to
later. Thus our interest in Vietnam was born in the post-World
War II period and motivated by concern for unchecked communist
movement into insecure and unstable areas.

More specifically, in 1947, President Truman announced a
national policy that pledged us to the unconditional support of
"free people who are resisting attempted subjugation by minorities
or by outside pressures." Congress approved that doctrine by a
large majority. That was the first benchmark along an unwitting
and precarious route. Then, in 1950, President Truman sent a military mission to Saigon. Later President Dwight Eisenhower and
Secretary of State Foster Dulles emphasized the policy of containment in association with a "massive retaliation" strategy and the
defeat of Premier Khrushchev's call for "wars of national liberation." Senator John F. Kennedy said in 1956 that "the cornerstone
of the free world is Southeast Asia." And when Senator Kennedy
was elected president, he demonstrated an interest in the so-called

---

*Karl von Clausewitz, born in 1780, served at an early age as a Prussian
soldier during the Napoleonic Wars. As the director of the Military Academy at Berlin from 1818 to 1830, he devoted his energy to promoting the
efficiency of the Prussian army and the strength of the Prussian state. His
famous work, *On War*, published in 1832 a year after his death, remains
the classic philosophical approach to military conflict.

small war concept. He became concerned about the size and readiness of the U.S. Army, which he thought had been neglected by President Eisenhower. Hence he increased the size of the army and personally sponsored the army's Green Berets. President Kennedy anticipated the advent of nuclear parity between the United States and the Soviet Union, where the two nuclear powers would, by virtue of both having such weapons, cancel out the nuclear threat. And after his confrontation with Khrushchev in Vienna in 1961, President Kennedy reportedly told Scotty Reston of the *New York Times*: "We have a problem in making our power credible, and Vietnam looks like the place."

Now this brief recounting emphasizes the multiple forces at work during those early years that led toward our involvement in Southeast Asia. That involvement was inevitable. President Kennedy set the tone of his administration in his inaugural address when he pledged our nation to "bear any burden, meet any hardship, support any friend, and oppose any foe to assure the survival and success of liberty." President Kennedy greatly increased our military effort in Vietnam with advisers, Green Berets, American-manned helicopters, and tactical aircraft.

But the young president in his zeal made a grievous mistake, in my opinion, in assenting to the overthrow of President Diem in South Vietnam. This action, in my opinion, morally locked us into the affairs of South Vietnam, since we were involved in changing the leadership of that country. There was no intention that Diem be killed, but he was.

Hence political chaos prevailed in South Vietnam for two years. I know that because I was there. We did not know who was running the country from day to day. It was like pushing a piece of spaghetti to get anything done. For the first time, our policy-makers gained an insight into the chronic internal problems of complex South Vietnam, a young country with no experience in self-government. If not for our involvement in the change of leadership in Saigon (and alternatively based on pragmatic considerations), we could have gracefully withdrawn our support from South Vietnam in view of a demonstrated lack of political unity in that small country. But that was not in the cards because in the wake of Kennedy's inaugural pronouncements, it is doubtful if his and Johnson's administrations would have risked the political repercussions. Kennedy's inaugural address was still ringing in the ears of Americans. On the other hand, strategic considerations associated with the strategic importance of Southeast Asia were still present. I refer, of course, to the oil of Indonesia, to the tin and rubber of Malaysia, and particularly to the narrow waterways to the Indian Ocean, known as seaway "choke points."

President Johnson inherited the problem. He was obsessed with his Great Society program. No one "bore a burden or met a hardship" except those on the battlefields and their loved ones. There was no question about our national objective. It was bipartisan, but the strategy was another matter. There was no agreement. It was based on wishful thinking and some faulty assumptions, particularly as to the nature of the threat and the character of the leadership in Hanoi. Specifically, there was a misjudgment as to the basic threat. The conventional wisdom in Washington was that the threat was a home-grown communist insurgency supported by guerrillas. And the counter to that was pacification. Now indeed, that was a significant element and pacification was important, but South Vietnam was not to be conquered by the guerrilla. It was to be conquered by the North Vietnamese army. The will and toughness of the leadership in Hanoi were greater than expected. A bombing campaign was intended to break that will, but restraint on the exercise of our capability, namely our air power, to break that will, was too much and it was lifted too late.

Our air campaign was constrained by three considerations: first, a fear of bringing the Chinese to the battlefield; second, a fear of escalating and geographically expanding the war, thereby involving other countries. One of the first official policy statements by President Johnson was that we would not expand the war. And finally, there was a fear of arousing further the well-organized antiwar elements at home and abroad. Also, our policymakers were influenced by our Korean War experience. They recalled General MacArthur's initiative in moving to the Yalu River along the Chinese border on the assumption that the Chinese army would not join the war. But the Chinese army moved en masse, and we found our troops forced back across the 38th parallel.

In 1953, the enemy was brought to the conference table allegedly, but I believe factually, by President Eisenhower's diplomatic threat to use nuclear weapons. At that time, the enemy had no counter to that threat. Our leadership in Vietnam and our political leadership at home had no such leverage in Vietnam physically or psychologically, since we did not have a monopoly on nuclear weapons. Also, we fought the war in Korea under the aegis of the United Nations. Hence our forces in Korea were under the United Nations Command. Our troops even now in Korea are under the aegis of the United Nations. We had no such posture during the Vietnam War. The United Nations was not involved in Vietnam and did not intend to get involved, and therefore we fought under our own aegis and not that of the collective United Nations.

There was wishful thinking by our policymakers that the western border of South Vietnam adjoining Laos and Cambodia would by protected by the Geneva Accords of 1954 and the Geneva Agreement on Laos of 1962.* Both of these agreements were to be policed by the International Control Commission, referred to as the ICC. The ICC was chaired by the Indian ambassador with membership from Poland and Canada. The assumption that the ICC would police adherence to the Geneva Accords of 1954 and the Geneva Agreement on Laos of 1962 was erroneous. The enemy freely used Laos and Cambodia, which turned South Vietnam into a battlefield with an open hostile flank of about 800 miles. U.S. troops were not allowed to cross the border until President Nixon permitted it on one occasion. That brief attack across the border was successful in destroying huge quantities of enemy supplies in Cambodia. In contrast, Korea was a peninsula with flanks on the sea. The Korean front along the 38th parallel was only about 150 miles.

Now I will turn to the second criterion listed by Karl von Clausewitz. Did we have the appropriate operational instruments? In other words, did we have the military forces trained and equipped for the task? Did we have the proper weapons and means of transportation? We did, thanks to our peacetime military forces. Among other things, our peacetime army recognized the capability and utility of the helicopter and foresaw the role and capability of the enemy guerrilla. Without the helicopter with its multiple uses, we could never have accomplished what we did in Vietnam, a country as long as California and half as wide. And with that long, hostile flank, which I referred to earlier, the helicopter gave us unprecedented battlefield mobility. The veterans in the audience remember well the utility of that vehicle. Roads were few and far between in Vietnam, and the very rugged terrain shifts from swamps to mountains. Also, I should point out that the army

---

*When John F. Kennedy entered the White House in January 1961, communist rebels were attempting to oust a conservative regime in Laos. President Kennedy decided to seek a negotiated settlement rather than to intervene in Laos with American troops. The Geneva Agreement, signed on 23 July 1962, stipulated that Laos would be neutralized under a coalition government representing communist as well as conservative elements.

started counterinsurgency training in anticipation of guerrilla warfare in the mid-1950s, and that gave us a head start on dealing with the enemy.

Now I would remind you that, unlike the French who fought the Vietnamese for a number of years, the American military suffered no loss like the destruction of Group Mobile 100 along Highway 19 in 1954 or like the defeat at Dien Bien Phu—a disaster for the French. The American soldiers, sailors, marines, airmen, and coastguardsmen were first-rate. I was and am proud of them. Army and marine troops had the task on the ground, working with the South Vietnamese military, to counter the guerrillas, to defeat the Vietcong Main Force Units and the North Vietnamese army, and to provide security for the people. The air force provided air support to our ground troops and bombed military targets in the north and in Laos. The bombing campaign in the north was designed to affect the morale and the will of the enemy leadership in Hanoi and was under the commander-in-chief, Pacific, and not myself. But I had first priority in using tactical aircraft as required to support our ground troops, a matter that I insisted upon. The navy took the fight to the enemy on the major waterways, particularly the Mekong and the Bassac rivers and the Cua Viet River south of the Demilitarized Zone (DMZ).* The navy also blocked the infiltration of enemy men and supplies by the sea and also provided naval gunfire support for our ground troops, particularly the marines in the north. The marines were in the northern part of the country, the army troops were in the center and the south.

The United States fighting men of all the services did an excellent job under difficult circumstances. They did not lose a single battle of consequence. But I must say, they were frustrated, as was I, because we were not allowed to pursue the enemy into Laos or Cambodia. The enemy was not so restrained. Many of you may not know that when South Vietnam was taken over by the North Vietnamese army, American combat troops had departed some two years earlier. That is very important, and everybody should know it, but there are many people in this country who do not.

The dedicated student and renowned expert on the Vietnamese communists, Professor Douglas Pike of the University of

---

*The Geneva Accords of 1954 established a Demilitarized Zone (DMZ) to serve as a buffer area for five miles on each side of the seventeenth parallel separating North Vietnam and South Vietnam. The negotiators at Geneva provided for the regrouping of Vietminh forces above and French forces below the demarcation line along the seventeenth parallel.

California at Berkeley has written: "The American military performance in Vietnam was particularly impressive. American troops won every significant battle that they fought, a record virtually unparalleled in the history of warfare."

Now Clausewitz's final advice for success in war was support of the war by the passions of the people. Another Clausewitz dictum comes to mind: "War is the extension of politics by other means." Vietnam was a war that continues to have an impact on politics. I fear that one of the big losses, in fact, probably the most serious loss of that war, is what I refer to as the Vietnam psychosis. Any time anybody brings up the thought that military forces might be needed, you hear the old hue and cry "another Vietnam, another Vietnam." That can be a real liability to us as we look to the future.

Needless to say, public attitudes did have a major influence during the Vietnam War years, not only on the conduct of the war but also on its outcome. Also, those negative attitudes influenced the morale of those of us on the battlefield.

What were the factors, developments, and politics that shaped the passions of the people? There were many. It was not a declared war, which made it impossible, under the law, to restrain people like Jane Fonda and Ramsey Clark and others who successfully and seriously divided support for our idealistic commitment articulated by President Kennedy and others. The Gulf of Tonkin Resolution passed by Congress in August 1964*, gave the president a carte blanche to do what he deemed necessary after one of our navy ships had reportedly been hit in international waters off the coast of North Vietnam. The Gulf of Tonkin Resolution, in my opinion, should have been reaffirmed each year, bringing about a public debate on the continuation of our commitment. There was apparently a political fear of such debate being initiated by the president or by Congress. If the resolution had been debated and reaffirmed every year, however, perhaps our country could have been more unified.

---

*North Vietnamese torpedo boats opened fire on an American destroyer in the Gulf of Tonkin on 2 August 1964, and two days later the American destroyer reported that it was again under attack. In retaliation, President Johnson ordered American planes to bomb patrol boat bases and oil storage depots in North Vietnam. On 7 August 1964, by a vote of 416–0 in the House and 88–2 in the Senate, Congress passed the Gulf of Tonkin Resolution authorizing the president "to take all necessary measures to repel any armed attack against the forces of the United States and to prevent further aggression."

There was disappointment that the SEATO Treaty—the Southeast Asia Treaty Organization*—could not protect our western battle flank and that the countries in Southeast Asia would not join with us in fighting against the communists. It was disillusioning to our people to observe that the SEATO Treaty had no teeth. It was a facade.

Also, the American people saw the war through the lens of World War II, where there were two front lines, the Americans on one side and the Germans on the other side in Europe, and the Japanese on the other side in Asia. World War II was a front-line war that could be followed on the map. But in Vietnam that was impossible because there was no apparent geographic war objective for the people reading the newspaper and trying to follow the war. We had far too few troops to fight a linear war. This became perplexing and frustrating to our people.

The policy of deferring college students from the draft destabilized the campuses and developed a psychological atmosphere that played into the hands of the antiwar factions in the United States and the communists in Hanoi. Finally, the cost of pursuing an ambiguous strategy exceeded the stamina of a substantial percentage of our body politic.

The Tet Offensive† by the North Vietnamese communists was never perceived in perspective by the American people. A strategic counterattack like the Tet Offensive of early February 1968 is a reaction by the enemy to the recognized failure of its strategy. The North Vietnamese strategy had not been successful and had to be changed. That brought about the Tet Offensive. Unfortunately, some reported that the Tet Offensive was a manifestation of the enemy's success. The enemy, of course, was able to attack along that long western flank, whereas we were unable to anticipate fully where he was going to attack, making defense of the western flank virtually impossible. But, thanks to the helicopter, we were able to

---

*The Southeast Asia Treaty Organization (SEATO) was created in 1954 as a regional defense pact for the South Pacific. The United States officially joined the organization when the Senate ratified the treaty by an 82–1 vote. The members agreed to consultations in the event of political or military emergencies, but they did not promise to commit combat forces to defend the status quo in Southeast Asia.

†Tet is the most important Vietnamese festival and celebrates the lunar new year. On 30 January 1968, on the eve of the Tet holidays, the Vietcong launched attacks against urban areas throughout South Vietnam. While North Vietnamese soldiers were engaging American forces in diversionary operations in the Central Highlands and northern border areas, Vietcong units assaulted thirty-six provincial capitals and five major cities in South Vietnam.

react to the enemy's initiatives. Yet, the Tet Offensive was pronounced by Walter Cronkite and others as evidence that we were losing in the south. The fact that the Tet Offensive occasioned no public uprising by the people of South Vietnam against the Saigon regime was a significant factor, particularly since the communists publically announced that there were going to be massive uprisings. Indeed, the communist Tet Offensive was a political defeat for Hanoi, but that perspective was given very little public visibility in the United States. In contrast to World War II and the Korean War, there was no media censorship imposed in Vietnam. Also Vietnam was American's first—indeed, the world's first— war covered by television. Many journalists reported irresponsibly and against the interests of political success. For the first time, many who reported on the war were not American citizens. To me, it is unconscionable for our own media to be indifferent, as many reporters were, when our country sends its troops to war. Finally, certain television personalities had more influence on the public by their pronouncements than informed and responsible senior public officials. That is a strange quirk in the nature and development of our democracy.

The matter of censorship in Vietnam is an interesting subject, but I shall not dwell here on why it was not imposed. But let me say that studies of the matter at the time indicated that, although it could only be imposed by the South Vietnamese government, we would, in effect, have had to take over that complicated task. And finally, the circumstances would be such that censorship could have been undercut in a matter of days by smuggling news stories and film out of the country to a nearby city of a noninvolved country from which the story could be filed.

But there were also other developments that stirred the passions of people. Webster's Dictionary defines passion as an emotion that is "stirring and ungovernable." President Johnson's announcement on 31 March 1968 not to run for reelection was reported as a decision brought about because of the enemy's Tet Offensive. This has been mentioned so often that most people consider it a fact. It is not a fact. I was visiting with President Johnson on an evening in November 1967. I had been called back to Washington and invited to stay at the White House. (When one is invited to stay at the White House, one accepts.) The president and I were talking in the late evening. He said, "I want to tell you something that Lady Bird, Lynda, and Luci know and only one other person." Then he said, "I trust you and I want to get your reaction." He said, "I don't think I will run for reelection." And I said, "Mr. President, why is that?" He said, "I am a sick man." He said, "I've got more things wrong with me than you can imagine." He then reflected on President Eisenhower, who had had a coronary attack when he was president. He reflected on the fact that President Woodrow Wilson had been an invalid for a period of his presidency. He pointed out that our laws did not permit the transfer of executive power. (That has now been changed in recent years.) Then he said, "It is unfair to the American people to have other than a healthy president, and I am not a healthy man." Of course, as you know, he died shortly after he had left office.

The perceived context of the president's announcement and the way it was handled by the media created a lessening of support for the war. They blamed his resignation on the Tet Offensive, which they seemed to consider a defeat for the United States. It was clear that they had misjudged the event some weeks later. Then the assassination of Martin Luther King added another dimension to the emotions of the body politic, putting it on the verge of the ungovernable. And then came Watergate, and we saw the systematic withdrawal of our troops following the signing of the so-called Paris Peace Agreement,* which was theoretically workable but practically had little if any chance of success.

About two years after the withdrawal of all U.S. and allied combat troops, the North Vietnamese army came south with sixteen divisions and attacked on a broad front. The South Vietnamese forces were in a very difficult position because of the extensive western flank with Laos and Cambodia and because we had not given them the military supplies we had promised. One of the reasons for that was because during the Yom Kippur War, we opened our warehouses to replace Israeli equipment destroyed by the Egyptian attack. And finally, we observed in mid-1973 the Case-Church Amendment to the fiscal 1974 appropriation act which prohibited any American funds whatsoever from being used "to finance directly or indirectly combat activities by United States military forces in or over or from off the shore of North Vietnam, South Vietnam, Laos and Cambodia." This was an unambiguous message to the communist leaders in Hanoi that they could break the Paris Peace Accord and we would not react.

---

*Formally signed on 25 February 1973, the Paris Peace Agreement arranged for a cease-fire in Vietnam and an exchange of war prisoners. General elections were to be held to pave the way for the eventual reunification of Vietnam. But while requiring the complete withdrawal of American and allied forces from Indochina, the peace agreement did not demand the removal of North Vietnamese troops from South Vietnam.

We have since learned from General Dung, who commanded the North Vietnamese forces that came down two years after we had withdrawn and took over the south, that Watergate played a role in the timing of the attack that amounted to the breaking of the Paris Agreement. The enemy realized that Watergate had paralyzed us politically and therefore, there would be no American reaction to their attack. So the Paris Peace Agreement was broken. Massive communist troops from North Vietnam invaded and conquered the south after the United States had paralyzed itself.

Now what can we learn from the Vietnam experience? Indeed, I believe that our political leaders must be more cautious in making commitments to foreign countries. Our determination of strategy in Washington must be more thorough in its research and examination, and in the process the military should have a stronger voice in the development of strategic decisions. It would seem to me that the greatest challenge of our cherished democracy is to heed another dictum of Sun Tzu: "The supreme excellence in subduing an enemy is to defeat him without having to fight him." In other words, defeat him politically and psychologically. It seems to me that our lawmakers could pass a measure, short of declaration of war, that would restrain efforts to undermine our constitutionally determined national objectives and weaken our resolve. It is not in our national interest to have news commentators, who are easily panic-stricken, pose as secretary of state or even as president and pronounce national policy. There needs to be public pressure to force those father figures of television to report the news and not make the news. President Johnson made a shocking statement when he said that when he lost Walter Cronkite, he lost the American people. Can you imagine a commentator or script reader having that much clout or power?

Can our cherished, open, democratic society cope with future challenges without responsible and self-disciplined mass media? Will it take another Pearl Harbor? It is interesting to speculate about the turn of events in World War II if it had not been for the galvanizing and unifying effect of Pearl Harbor on the American public.

In the long stretch of history, our actions in Southeast Asia will probably look different from our views so close to the events that occurred just over a decade ago. Even now the ASEAN countries (ASEAN stands for Association of Southeast Asian Nations) see the war in a different perspective from our own. Specifically, we are talking about the Philippines, Indonesia, Malaysia, Singapore, and Thailand. All of those countries have been colonies of the west except Thailand. Those are the countries of Southeast Asia outside of Indochina. All of Indochina is now Hanoi's empire, consisting of North and South Vietnam, Laos, and Cambodia. All are dominated militarily with Vietnamese troops on the ground. The ASEAN countries say that from their viewpoint, America won. The United States won by holding the line against communist expansion which bought ten years for them to mature and to gain confidence in running their own affairs, since they had until recently been colonies of Western powers, with the exception of Thailand. Also, the American military effort bought time for those countries to improve their infrastructure and their economies and to develop resistance against communist pressures. Meanwhile, those countries of Southeast Asia have looked toward Indochina dominated by Hanoi, and they have seen the boat people, the concentration camps, and the invasion of Cambodia. They have seen the unhappy population of Indochina—nobody wants to go there anymore—many want to leave and are trying to do so. They have seen the poor state of the communist-dominated economy in Indochina, and they have concluded that they want no part of that system.

I was asked several years ago to make a talk in New Delhi, India, at an international conference. There were representatives from most, if not all, of the ASEAN countries, and they told me what I have just told you. From their standpoint, we won. They said that we saved them because we held the line for ten years, and they pointed out that Indonesia would never have thrown the Russians out in 1966 if we had not made a commitment to South Vietnam.

But on the other side of the coin, the loss of Cam Ranh Bay gives the Russians, for the first time, an excellent naval and air base south of the 17th parallel, the largest they have outside of the Soviet Union. But the communist government in Vietnam, which has demonstrated an inability to run the huge territory it has militarily conquered, is not necessarily a permanent fixture. It is a government in serious trouble. The communist rulers have created an economic disaster in Indochina, and we, in my opinion, should not bail them out. But we also should remind ourselves that they are very clever people.

I would like to put a postscript on my remarks, and it will probably preempt a question. I understand there is a movie out called *Platoon*. Many of you in the audience may have seen that movie. I have not. I have talked to many veterans and I have received a number of letters about it. Apparently the producers of this film made a list of all the illegal and improper things that happened in Vietnam associated with American soldiers. Then they developed a film in which they included all those illegal, immoral, and unauthorized acts into one platoon over a period of several months. That is absurd. Things took place in Vietnam that were against regulations and against humanity. But they were not commonplace. They were isolated. However, I understand this film conveys the impression that this was typical of a platoon, that these illegal and criminal actions were commonplace and condoned. There were more than a million men who served in Vietnam during my four and a half years there, and there were a number of crimes reported. There were crimes against civilians and crimes against fellow soldiers. And in a *city* of 500,000 (which was about our maximum troop strength during the course of the war), you are going to have some bad actors, you are going to have some illegal acts, and you are going to have crimes, but they will not happen in every block in the city. They will be spread over a period of time throughout the whole population.

During my four and a half years in Vietnam, there were thirty-one men who were tried for the murder of civilians. There were seventeen that were tried for rape, and eleven that were tried for manslaughter. Of the fifty-nine that were tried, thirty-six were convicted by a military court.

I am disturbed that the movie *Platoon* seems to be derogatory to *all* Vietnam veterans. I believe that many who see it will think that it depicts actions in Vietnam that were typical, and that such atrocious acts were tolerated. In reality, however, illegal and immoral acts were detected and reported and dealt with. I think the uninitiated, the average person who sees the film, will view it as typical of the performance of the American soldier in Vietnam, which is unfair and false.

QUESTION: You talked about how the media apparently distorted the record of the war, and it seemed to me that the media reported on a lot of things that were official government policy but which the government would have preferred not disclosing. I will cite two examples. I would like to know whether you feel the media distorted these: (1) the aspect of the pacification program called "Project Phoenix" and (2) the secret war in Cambodia.

ANSWER: The "Project Phoenix" was designed and executed by the CIA. It was designed to capture the communist political leaders, the so-called infrastructure. It was designed to capture and interrogate them and try to identify the whole gamut of the political infrastructure. It was not intended as an assassination program. There is evidence that there were some illegal assassinations, but they were certainly not tolerated. But that was not the intent. It does not make any sense to assassinate an individual who has information that you need in order to try to identify the whole political structure.

The "secret war" in Cambodia happened while I was in Washington. There was bombing in Cambodia along the border by B-52s before it was announced to the public. And this was done really as a concession to Prince Norodom Sihanouk. He transmitted a message to the effect that if there were North Vietnamese troops on his soil, he would not object to them being bombed as long as it was not made public and did not become international news. Otherwise, Prince Sihanouk thought that it would be detrimental to his relations with the communist governments. Sihanouk was very insecure. There were many strikes on North Vietnamese military positions inside of Cambodia that were not made public. I do not know of any other war related to your question about Cambodia other than the air war. I was not in Vietnam at the time, but as I reflect on my days in Washington, the Cambodian army frequently asked for air support, and it was frequently made available to them. I believe that was public knowledge.

QUESTION: What are your thoughts on the fall of Saigon in 1975 and our absolute refusal to act, especially considering that the offensive tactics of the North Vietnamese army could have been greatly retarded by tactical air strikes?

ANSWER: When the peace treaty was broken by the North Vietnamese army and the communists overran South Vietnam with sixteen divisions, we did not react. Actually, the military and the administration did not have the authority to react because of the Case-Church Amendment to the 1974 appropriations act passed in mid-1973 which said that no military force could be used on land, sea, or air, on or off the shore of North Vietnam, South Vietnam, Laos, or Cambodia. So it was an act of Congress that overrode the authority of the president to react. Gerald R. Ford was president at the time. When I went to see him to talk about the matter, he said that his hands were tied. The communists were very clever. As I pointed out in my earlier remarks, the timing of their attack was associated with the Watergate episode, which they thought had divided and virtually paralyzed the country, in addition to the Case-Church Amendment. And as I pointed out before, we had given the South Vietnamese only one half of the military supplies, spare parts, petroleum, and ammunition that we had promised them. So they had to ration bullets—I think six bullets per rifleman per day or something like that, and only a few 81mm mortar rounds per tube as an example. Thus the South Vietnam army was in a no-win situation.

QUESTION: I have heard that there were seven soldiers behind the lines for every one at the front. Is that true?

ANSWER: That is an exaggeration, but with the responsibility of our supporting logistically our forces plus all of the Vietnamese forces, the Korean forces, the Thai forces, the pacification program, and maintaining the helicopters, quite a number of people were required behind the fighting troops. The ratio of support to fighting troops in Vietnam was really, even considering those circumstances, little, if at all, greater than during World War II. A seven-to-one ratio is inaccurate.

QUESTION: Do you feel, while you were in command, that the United States was winning the war, and could you define "winning the war?"

ANSWER: My frequent statement was that we were making progress. "Winning the war" in a traditional sense is ambiguous. As you may know, if you were there—and I gather you are a veteran—we were on the learning curve for several years, but the troops and their commanders, I think, learned quite fast. And as I said in my earlier remarks, they did not lose a battle of any consequence despite the fact that we had that wide-open flank to the west. Now after the Tet Offensive, the enemy was clobbered, and it was very clear at that time that we had the upper hand as we had never had it before. What I wanted to do at that time was to step up the bombing, hopefully get authority to pursue the enemy into Cambodia, cut the Ho Chi Minh Trail,* and make an amphibious and airborne hook north of the Demilitarized Zone, taking the fight to the enemy in the north. I also wanted to bomb military targets in North Vietnam as President Nixon did in 1972. If such bombing had been executed in 1968 and had been associated with a new aggressive strategy, I think the enemy would have come to the conference table. You have to realize that we did not intend to

---

*The North Vietnamese sent troops and equipment down a series of primitive trails winding through the mountains and jungles of Laos and Cambodia and emptying into South Vietnam. In 1964, the North Vietnamese began expanding this so-called Ho Chi Minh Trail into a sophisticated logistical network capable of handling heavy trucks and other vehicles.

unify the two countries through the use of force. We wanted to save South Vietnam from being taken over by North Vietnam, and that meant that we wanted to bring the enemy to the conference table and negotiate a settlement, as was done in Korea. Our goal was to preserve the integrity and the freedom of South Vietnam.

QUESTION: You have offered a very complicated explanation for why we lost the war in Vietnam, ranging from the mistake in deposing of President Diem in the south all the way to the need to resupply the Israelis in the Yom Kippur War. I wonder if you would entertain a much simpler theory: that people in an open democratic society like the United States recognized, in a series of cumulative events, that our military and political leaders were wrong, that they had embarked on a war that had no real purpose, and that they were prepared to sacrifice the lives of tens of thousands of Americans and millions of dollars in our treasury for a pointless war. Would you entertain that alternative explanation?

ANSWER: Well, I understand exactly what you are saying, but I think you have to put this in the context of how we got into the war in the first place, and I have tried to explain that process. Our intentions were very honorable. Our intentions were consistent with policies that evolved after World War II. It is quite understandable how those policies evolved, and after they had evolved, those of us in the military wanted to make good the commitment. What you are saying is that the commitment was not worth making good, and that is a judgment, of course. That is your judgment, and it is probably shared by some, perhaps many, in the country. But nevertheless the fact is that we were committed, and why we were committed goes back to the factors that I mentioned in the early part of my remarks. But you are quite right. It is very complicated.

QUESTION: You mentioned that it was in keeping with the commitment made by President Truman and continued through President Eisenhower and President Kennedy that the United States made a noble commitment to Vietnam. You also, however, mentioned in the beginning of your talk that perhaps Kennedy felt that the United States was losing some credibility militarily and that Southeast Asia would be a good region to flex our muscle. Do you feel that the United States had exhausted, prior to embarking upon a military campaign in Vietnam, all other alternative actions? For example, is it not true that Ho Chi Minh did not want to go to the communists and actually tried to approach the United States, and to what extent did the United States respond before making military commitments?

ANSWER: Well, I suppose you could rewrite history along the lines that you suggest. Whether they are supported by the facts, I do not know. Of course, I have heard that that was the disposition of Ho Chi Minh. But I am not at all convinced that such was the case. Communists do not change their spots overnight, and I do not think Ho Chi Minh was about to do that. On the other hand, I am familiar with that school of thought. But, yes, you can go back and rewrite all kinds of history. We study history, and as we get further and further away from an event, it begins to come into a sharper focus. A lot of our dealings with foreign countries have not yet been made public.

I do know that President Johnson and his administration tried desperately to get the enemy to come to the conference table, working through ambassadors in Yugoslavia, Hungary, and other satellite communist countries of Eastern Europe. The enemy finally came to the conference table in Paris four years after the Tet Offensive. And then after four years of squabbling, they really decided only one thing and that was the shape of the conference table. We gave them no incentive to do otherwise. Finally, Secretary of State Kissinger made concessions, some of which I thought were not justified, which put the South Vietnamese in a very awkward position. The South Vietnamese were in a very tenuous position as a result of the concessions made in Paris.

My school of thought, which I have already related, is that after the defeat of the Tet Offensive—and there is no arguing about that any more, it was a disaster for the enemy—our bombing capability could have been exercised as it was in 1972 and early 1973. Then I think they would have come to the conference table, and we could have negotiated from a position of strength. The British consul in Hanoi in 1966 and 1967, John Colvin, wrote a revealing article about four or five years ago in the *Washington Quarterly.* Colvin was in day-to-day contact with officials of the communist government in Hanoi, and he stated the opinion that the communist leaders in Hanoi were on the verge of capitulation in late 1967 because of the effectiveness of our bombing, even though it was not a full-scale operation. If there is merit to that, certainly the type of bombing that President Nixon delivered in 1972, if delivered four years earlier, on top of the defeat of the Tet Offensive, could have been very significant.

QUESTION: General Westmoreland, sir. This is Sergeant Turner, I am retired from the army, sir. I have not been in an audience with the General since 1953 in the Kumhwa Valley, when we pulled out of Korea and went back to Japan. Since that time, I served one tour with you in Vietnam; I also served in 1961 and in 1963. I have three years in Vietnam, and I appreciate your statement here tonight about the way that the private American soldier fought that war and fought it well and won it. And anyone who thinks that that little grunt out there did not win that war had better look at some humanitarian kinds of things that were done in Vietnam that you do not hear about: orphanages were taken care of; food and clothes and contacts in the United States were taken care of. The United States Army fought that fight in the most humanitarian way that that war could be fought. Now that is a contradiction in terms, but that is the way it happened.

ANSWER: Thank you.

QUESTION: The question that I have for you, General, arises from our experience in Vietnam, where a lot of us served. As I look around the crowd, I see many kids here who were our age when we were there. But my question is: In your thinking pertaining to Honduras and Nicaragua and other Latin American countries, what is going to happen down there and what should we be watching and saying to the politicians to keep that from happening?

ANSWER: It is a very good question and a very timely one. We do not hear much about the strategic importance of that part of the world. Central America and the Caribbean Basin are far more important to us strategically than Southeast Asia. More than 50 percent of our shipping goes through the Gulf of Mexico. The Soviets have a submarine base, an army brigade, surface-to-air missiles, and aircraft landing almost every day in Cuba. Now that capability is being expanded to Nicaragua. From Nicaragua where are they going? Is the strategy of the communists to move toward the Panama Canal and dominate Panama, which could close the Panama Canal? Strategically, we could find ourselves bottled up. During World War II, between the bombing of Pearl Harbor on 7 December 1941 and 1 August 1942, there were about one hundred and fifty ships sunk by three Nazi submarines that were based in Germany but on station in the Atlantic. The number of ships that they damaged or sank was absolutely staggering. With the enemy, or our would-be enemy, controlling islands and pieces of real estate along a main route of communication through the Panama Canal and from the Gulf of Mexico, we could find ourselves in a position where we would be unable to defend Western Europe with American troops if the need arose. Now, of course, we hope that the posture of our army in Europe is such that we can deter any such attack, and I am not suggesting that the Russians are on the verge of such an attack. I think that the communist strategy is to try to intimidate the countries of Western Europe and break up NATO, but I think we always have to look at our real capabilities and to think more in strategic terms. No, we do not want the Soviets to increase their hegemony any further in that part of the world. How do we stop that in view of the Vietnam psychosis, which some of the questions have reflected tonight? Are we going to say that we will never use military force again? Can we get pushed around and let our enemies take over Panama, Costa Rica, other countries, other islands in the Caribbean, and yet not respond as we did in Granada? Are we going to give them a carte blanche to move as they see fit and bottle us up on our south flank? And the answer is: We are not going to do that. But we cannot rule out the use of military force. We hope we will not have to use it, but we must have it ready to use if necessary.

QUESTION: You have commented about the lack of support for the war among the American people and the effect that had on the war. You have not mentioned the lack of support for our side in the war that was evident among the South Vietnamese people. I am not referring to the political leaders, who clearly did not have the support of the average Vietnamese citizen. The average peasant in South Vietnam evidently did not support our side in the war. I propose to you that if the average Vietnamese citizen had supported our side in the war, that perhaps the outcome would have been different. Would you please comment?

ANSWER: Well, in my opinion, which is based on over four years of experience in Vietnam, the vast majority of the peasants in South Vietnam wanted no part of communist domination. And in view of what they have suffered, now nobody wants to go there, everybody wants to leave, the economy is a mess. They see first hand what has happened to them under a communist regime. Now you are making the statement, and I do not know what you base this on, that the average peasant was supporting the communist. I do not buy that at all. And my experience does not support that in the least.

# EDWARD N. LUTTWAK

Edward N. Luttwak was born on 4 November 1942 in Arand, Romania. After receiving a B.S. in 1964 from the London School of Economics and Political Science, he embarked upon an extraordinarily diversified and distinguished career. Luttwak worked in Eastern Europe for CBS television from 1964 to 1965, and then he returned to England to lecture at the University of Bath. After serving as an oil consultant in London between 1967 and 1968, he came to the United States to work as a strategic consultant in Washington, D.C. Then Luttwak went to Israel to serve as the deputy director of the Middle East Study Group in Jerusalem from 1970 to 1972, and he returned to the United States to serve an an associate director of the Washington Center of Foreign Policy Research between 1972 and 1975. Since receiving a Ph.D. in 1975 from The Johns Hopkins University, Luttwak has served as a senior fellow at the Center for Strategic and International Studies at Georgetown University.

Luttwak has written numerous scholarly books, which cover a remarkable range of subjects. His publications include the following: *Coup D'Etat*, 1968; *A Dictionary of Modern War*, 1971; *The Strategic Balance*, 1972; *The Political Uses of Sea Power*, 1974; *The U.S.-U.S.S.R. Nuclear Weapons Balance*, 1974; (with Dan Horowitz) *The Israeli Army*, 1975; *The Grand Strategy of the Roman Empire: From the First Century A.D. to the Third*, 1976; *Strategy and Politics: Collected Essays*, 1980; *The Grand Strategy of the Soviet Union*, 1983; *The Pentagon and the Art of War: The Question of Military Reform*, 1984; *On the Meaning of Victory: Essays on Strategy*, 1986; and *Strategy: The Logic of War and Peace*, 1987. Many of these works have been translated into various languages.

Luttwak has made a major contribution to the ongoing debate over the strategic issues confronting the United States since the Vietnam War. Besides contributing research papers to numerous collections, he has participated in many conferences dealing with national security questions. Luttwak has also tried to reach out and influence public thinking about military affairs. His articles have appeared regularly in *Esquire, The Times Literary Supplement, Commentary,* and other journals. Luttwak has not only been a strong advocate for military reform in the United States, but he has also frequently served as a defense consultant for the American government.

# THE IMPACT OF VIETNAM ON STRATEGIC THINKING IN THE UNITED STATES

## by Edward N. Luttwak

**M**y subject is the impact of Vietnam on American strategic thinking. When we speak of strategy or the strategic, we are speaking of conflict, and the first thing to note is that conflict inherently has different levels. There is a technical level—the level of machines. If we consider, for example, the Strategic Defense Initiative—whether to talk about it, analyze it, or implement it—we cannot do so without contending with the technical level. Ultimately, no matter whether the scheme is a good idea politically or not, the fact is that machines have to work. If the machines will not work, SDI will not work. If one wants to argue about SDI, therefore, one has to know about the technical level.

But that is only the beginning. There is a tactical level of conflict too, and it is present in space as well as on land. If you favor SDI and perceive it as potentially very useful, then you must explain how it is going to work tactically, that is, in combat. How would space stations, or whatever the equipment is, attack ballistic warheads coming in without being attacked in turn? How would they evade attack or attack the attackers? When one deals with tactics, one must deal not only with locational or other material factors but also with the intangibles—if it is the infantry, for example, one must ask whether the soldiers will take cover when they are supposed to take cover and attack when they are supposed to attack. Moving becomes crucial. This then is the tactical level, the level of the use of equipment and the conduct of individuals and small units.

Above that, there is another level of fighting, the operational level. At that level, one is no longer looking at the single infantry platoon or how any one SDI battle station might attack ballistic warheads. Instead, one is considering the whole array of interactive forces, the whole SDI scheme with all the different combat elements, whatever they may be. Instead of focusing on the one platoon, thirty soldiers strung out along the ground, one is also seeing what is on their flanks, on their rear, and in direct support. Thus the operational level deals with the entirety of the forces in action.

Now, above the operational level, we have the highest, purely military level, the level of theater strategy. One is no longer asking what is happening to a platoon, a division, or even an army group, but rather what is happening to an entire territory that makes a reasonably self-contained whole. If one is fighting in northwest Europe or perhaps North Africa, what is happening to *all* the forces involved? In action, what one does has to be right at that level as well. To prevail brilliantly in battle at the operational level with one's forces need not save one from theater-level defeat—perhaps that victory would let the enemy come in with another force. If one is examining the SDI, one has to work out not only how battle stations would be used against ballistic warheads but also how the entire defense will work against cruise missiles as well. In this case, the theater defines a *category* of forces. What would be the use of building an SDI system to intercept every single ballistic warhead if there is no protection against manned aircraft skillfully flown and cruise missiles skillfully designed? In other words, if one is providing a strategic defense, one must provide the whole array that covers the whole theater of conflict.

So in strategy, therefore, we discover that there are four different levels of military action: the technical, the tactical, the operational, and the theater-strategic. If one is thinking strategy, one must do so concurrently on four levels. One understands immediately that in order to do anything right, to win, to succeed, one must be at least adequate at each of these levels, whereas one can fail by failing at just one level. If the machines will not work, whether they are rifles or SDI battle stations, it does not matter how wonderful one's tactics may be, what wonderful operational methods one may have prepared for the whole force or system, or how great the whole array is at the theater level. One can fail at every level, but to succeed one must succeed at each level. That is why strategy is more difficult than gardening and a great many other things.

Finally, there is one more level. We all know that strategy is not a game but an extension of state action. We know, therefore, that there is another level above all the military levels, and that is the level of grand strategy, where one encounters the expression of political choice. It could be a king, it could be a dictator, or it could be an elected assembly making the choice, but in any case, it dominates decisions. Let us assume that one has come up with an SDI that is technically brilliant: one has worked out all the tactics so that Soviet forces could not, in fact, attack the battle stations and neutralize them before they could fire. And one has worked out the operational method so that the system can be effective in terms of the whole force against the whole enemy force. And one has worked out the other elements, all the long-range nuclear missiles against all the Soviet long-range nuclear missiles. But it would all be for naught if the political decision makers would rather spend the money for ice cream. There is no logic of strategy, no rule that one may derive from it, that overcomes the political choice, whether it is made by a king, a dictator, or a democratic process. All analysis and all action are subject to the political choice.

There is also something else that one meets in grand strategy, and that is all the other instruments of state power, military and not. One may decide that SDI is wonderful technically, tactically, operationally, and at the theater level, and yet still decide that one does not want it, that one would rather have conventional forces. Why is that? Well, for one thing, at the level of grand strategy, one encounters state relationships with all other countries, allies, neutrals, and enemies. That is also where the national economy comes into the picture. The scheme may be wonderful but too costly. Finally, but most important, there is diplomatic interaction. Let us say that we are considering some missiles to be placed in Europe to achieve a certain balance meant to reassure our allies. But in the reality of diplomacy, our allies may say that they do not want these missiles. It could be for completely frivolous reasons. It could be because, let us say, a nuclear reactor has exploded in Chernobyl. A clumsy Ukrainian technician has dropped a wrench, there is a nuclear accident, and therefore Western public opinion rejected a nuclear system. After having splendidly designed a missile, after having worked out all the tactics and operational methods of its employment, one still fails to achieve one's purpose because of political circumstances. And what are political circumstances influenced by? Hard facts, yes, but also whims, transient ideas, delusions, and myths, and they too affect the reality of strategy.

In terms of our definition, there was no strategic thinking in the conduct of the Vietnam War. The fact is that if one went there to observe what was going on, one would encounter disparate, divergent activity. First of all, there was frenzied activity at the technical level. We, as a nation, were coming up with gadgets all the time, hoping that some new clever gadget would enable the United States to win the Vietnam War. For example, it was discovered that patrols were bumping into enemies in the jungle, and so the idea was born to develop gadgets that would sense human smell. Much decision making was not on *any* strategic level. Rather it was simply quantitative. General Westmoreland would ask Defense Secretary McNamara for another one hundred thousand men. McNamara might reply "yes" or "no." Or the president might say: "You cannot have one hundred thousand. I will give you eighty thousand." It was almost as if the war had been transformed into a quantitative activity in itself.

The underlying notion was that if one sent lots of air force squadrons that would fly lots of sorties and drop lots of bombs, if one deployed lots of field artillery battalions with lots of firepower—if one generated a lot of firepower, somehow one could win. When Westmoreland wanted another one hundred thousand men, his request was not frivolous. He wanted them because he wanted a certain number of artillery battalions, and a certain number of air squadrons, and so on, to generate more firepower. Unfortunately, the enemy, the Vietcong, and even the North Vietnamese, stubbornly refused to assemble in conveniently targetable massed formations. They kept dispersing, making the industrial output of firepower largely irrelevant. A field artillery battalion from the United States could be "processing" ammunition by the shipload without actually killing any Vietcong or North Vietnamese troops. Those four hundred and fifty American soldiers could have been carrying flutes instead of manning howitzers, and if they had just played their flutes, it would have had exactly the same effect on the outcome of the war.

The striking thing throughout the high-level discussions recorded in the Pentagon papers is that hardly anything was said about tactics. The tactical level was ignored. Westmoreland might say: "Give me another one hundred thousand men." McNamara might respond: "No, I am only going to give you eighty-five thousand." Nobody asked how those men were to fight. When a patrol made contact, if somebody opened fire on it in any way, the troops would hit the ground and call for artillery support, or air support, or both. Even with marvelous communications, it would take several minutes before the shells would start landing. During those minutes, the Vietcong or North Vietnamese troops who had opened fire on the patrol would hit it with mortar rounds, inflict casualties, and then disperse. If only patrols had used proper tactics, namely normal tactics, the tactics that the United States Army used right through the Second World War, each contact would have been fought through with some result. The Vietcong were usually poor soldiers, they were always running out of ammunition and, if charged, would usually run away. But the tactical level was ignored. It was as if a homemaker said: "I want to improve the food that I cook. Send me another truckload of steak." And she would continue burning them. Nobody said: "You know, if you would just learn how to *cook*, that would do more for your food than asking for more truckloads of steak."

But what is the trick involved in this talk of tactics? The trick is that tactics are not really about how to do things. It is not the knowledge that one should charge instead of hitting the ground. We all know that. It is not the procedure. Remember, one is dealing with war. To do one thing rather than the other, it is not enough to learn a routine. One needs the morale and cohesion to do it. The unit has to be cohesive so that when one soldier decides to charge forward, the others will follow him—not because they believe in the war necessarily, but because they like the man, and they do not want to let him down. Cohesion and training and leadership make tactics, not procedure.

That brings me to the problem of officer leadership. If one sends young men to West Point for four years to study electrical engineering and management and to learn all the necessary skills to be promoted to general, they will not want to die in a nameless rice paddy. The one thing that McNamara never questioned was the fact that the army, for reasons of career management, insisted on one-year rotations for its career officers in order to give equal shares of exposure to career-enhancing combat. The lieutenant-colonels would all receive a turn in command of a battalion in combat. This would be very important in their files when it came time for promotion. There was one-year rotation in theory, but in practice many served for only six months. The effect on tactics may well be imagined. The commander would arrive in Vietnam fresh from Leavenworth or Germany. He would come with all the standard ideas in his head, and it would take him about six months to figure out what he should be doing. When he first arrives in Vietnam, he wants to show the battalion under him that he is a man with drive. So he orders his men to do this or that, and he gets soldiers killed without achieving the purpose. By the end of his tour, he learns what he should be doing. But the six months are up, off he goes, and a new commander comes in to make the same mistakes all over again.

McNamara criticized the military constantly. He questioned them constantly. He humiliated them constantly. The one thing he did not criticize was the one thing that would have made a difference at the level of tactics: experience. As the saying goes, we were not in Vietnam for ten years. We were in Vietnam for six months, twenty times over.

But, of course, tactics hardly matter if there is no operational method, no strategy to win. Westmoreland was in charge of MACV (Military Assistance Command, Vietnam). He was the man who was supposed to come up with the *method* for winning the war. A conceptual method. Do we want to secure the country? Or do we want to reduce the enemies in the field? If the purpose is to secure the country, what one needs is a militia, a country-wide home guard, with rapid-reaction forces to help out local militia units under attack. Instead of complete divisions with fifteen thousand men all kitted out to fight the Russians on the central European front, the forces should have been split up into small units, with each one left to defend a village while its militia was being formed. Of course, the Vietcong would gather to hit them one by one, but reaction forces could respond in turn. That would have been the operational method called "defending the territory against the bad guys" with American troops split up into local home guards and reaction forces ready to help each village when attacked. Perhaps one could have won the war that way, but it would have turned the United States Army into an Asian constabulary in permanence—to keep the war won year after year.

Another method would have been to kill the enemy. In that case, we might have said: "We are not here to defend the territory or the people. We are here to kill the enemy." Now the enemy was centered in North Vietnam, so we would have had to invade North Vietnam. Westmoreland now says that they would not have let him invade the north. But he never truly asked. He presided as the chairman of the board over a very diversified corporation, and he was a good chairman: he encouraged each department of the company to do the best that it could, concurrently. So the United

States economic assistance people (AID),* would come to a village in Vietnam and help it out, put in a new well, and so on. The next day the air force would bomb the village. Then a special-forces team would go in to work with the survivors to rebuild the village and train them in self-defense. Next the artillery would barrage the village. Then a psychological operations unit would pass around leaflets and explain the importance of fighting the Vietcong. Then the navy would flatten the place with its gunfire.

In Vietnam, it was fair shares for all. Each one of the different bureaucracies was trying hard to get a good share of the budget and of the promotions for its own officers. So the navy was present with its aerial bombing, surface gunfire, and coastal fleet. The marines did their bit. The army was there complete. There was armor in Vietnam, even though there were no fronts to smash and no Rommels† to outmaneuver. The artillery was there in huge numbers, even though the enemy refused to assemble so that it could be shelled properly. It was the administrative mentality, the corporate mentality that dominated MACV, with no recognition that to win a war one must first decide how to win. One needs first of all to make a deliberation at the level of grand strategy. Then one has to figure out how to achieve the goal of that grand strategy at the level of theater strategy. Then one must work out the operational methods to do so. And then one has to ensure that the tactics of each force are congruent and at least adequate. They do not have to be brilliant. But none of this happened in Vietnam.

One effect of the reappraisals of the Vietnam War is that this kind of level-by-level analysis is now understood. The United States Army now recognizes the operational level of war; it realizes that concepts of war and the art of war are not just the concerns of Clausewitz and other theorists.

Its levels aside, the core of strategy is that there is always an adversary present, an enemy, not just a competitor. He sees what you are doing, he studies it, he opposes it. He has his own means and his own intelligence. Everything done in strategy is an action that meets a reaction. Everything is governed by the presence of an

---

*The Agency for International Development (AID) oversees American technical and economic aid programs throughout the third world.

†Erwin Rommel, the leading German tank commander, headed the Afrika Korps during WWII. After winning fame as the "Desert Fox" in North Africa, Field Marshall Rommel commanded the German defense on the Western Front in Europe. He ultimately committed suicide after participating in an unsuccessful plot to assassinate Hitler.

enemy who watches and reacts. Now this simple fact has a very unsimple consequence: everything done in strategy evolves as a parabolic action. One starts doing something, and it goes well; one puts more effort into it, and it goes better. But then one reaches a culminating point of success, from which decline begins. If one is successful in civilian undertakings, what goes well can be improved with more effort. The action unfolds and expands. From one hamburger restaurant, one can reach the stage when there are five million McDonald outlets and the whole world is eating fast food. Actually, the success of the first fifty outlets makes the success of the fifty-first easier, it builds up McDonald's reputation and provides publicity for the business. But in strategy, matters are exactly opposite. In strategy, one can perhaps sneak by and open the first five or six outlets, but soon resistance builds up, and opening the seventh becomes very difficult. The eighth is impossible. If you insist on trying, bankruptcy is the result.

Let me explain what I mean. Consider weapons. You develop a weapon that is very effective, and it frightens the enemy. Now, what happens to the weapon? The enemy takes it very seriously because you have made a real breakthrough. He assigns a very high priority to developing measures with which to counter it. So this highly successful weapon encounters the result of all the efforts of the enemy to devise countermeasures. Let us say that you are trying to bomb Germany during the Second World War, and you develop a wonderful beam navigation device that directs bombers right over the target. Well, the Germans are alarmed. They focus their intelligence to find out what principle is involved. They interrogate prisoners of war and have their technicians devise countermeasures—all on the highest priority. Please note that if your beam device had not been so very successful, the enemy would not have been so alarmed by it. He would not have assigned highest priorities to oppose the device. Other things being equal, his countermeasures therefore would be less effective. In the final outcome, the second-rate device could therefore provide more useful service than the better device.

When action provokes a reaction, the outcome is not paralysis or immobility. There is instead a rise and decline. That, obviously, has very powerful consequences. Consider states at the level of grand strategy, say, an Italian city-state, Siena, for example. Siena becomes stronger, and its leaders think that they will be able to lord it over the whole of Tuscany. They defeat the neighboring town. Now if this were commerce, as with fast food, you would say: "Well, they have knocked off one town, and now they will knock off another." In the world of strategy, matters are different. Beyond the ring of neighboring city-states already hostile, there was another outer ring that was simply indifferent to Siena. They might or might not buy Sienese fashions or entertain its painters, but they are not afraid of Siena. Before Siena could not get to them, and it could not help them. Now, suddenly they see a threat, and they start mobilizing against Siena. Two towns that were fighting one another make peace: they are both frightened by Siena. They make an alliance against it. The rising state evokes a reaction that will prevent it from making linear gains from a steady effort. Instead, a culminating point is reached.

Consider today's Soviet Union. The United States Army has seventeen active-duty divisions and maybe forty divisions in all, including reservists who would really be shocked if they were called up in peacetime. The Soviet Union has two hundred divisions. In Moscow, they say: "What is all this talk about the Soviet army? It is Pentagon propaganda. True, we have two hundred divisions. But remember, we are surrounded. We have the Chinese to cope with, for a start. The Chinese do not like us, and we need fifty army divisions to face them. We have the Turks on our border, and they are part of the North Atlantic Treaty Organization. Also, we have to worry about Iran, and consequently we have twenty divisions facing the Iranians. We also have some five or six divisions bogged down in Afghanistan because the Afghans refuse to enjoy the benefits of progressive government. We even have to worry about the Finns, and they are pretty tough. You Americans have nothing to worry about, only us. We have to worry about everybody."

The Russian who says that is recounting the consequences of the spectacular success of the Soviet Union in making itself so powerful. The Soviet Union became so powerful that everybody around it became hostile. Hence it has reached a culminating point of success, unlike the restaurant chain that continues to build success upon success. In other words, *the logic of strategy is not linear but paradoxical.* If you want to succeed in it, you should do the wrong thing, not the right thing. If you want to attack an enemy, avoid the nice and straight road that goes directly to his capital city. Do not take that road. Why? Because it is the good road. Choose a bad road, go over the mountains. If you want to keep the army properly organized, everything should be done in daylight, parade out the forces, and do everything neatly. That is the way we try to operate in the civilian world. But if you want to win, you have to attack at night, even though the result is confusion, disorder, and inefficiency. But that is the way of catching the enemy by surprise and winning.

Now why is the good road bad? Because it is good. Why is that circuitous, narrow, and dangerous mountain road the good road? Because it is the bad route. In other words, if you have an enemy who is watching your every move, paradoxical action is the best action. That has many implications, as you can imagine. One very powerful implication is simply that efficiency is not a valid criterion. In civilian life, one wants efficiency. We seek it by standardizing, by striving for economies of scale, and so on. But in strategy, efficiency is not the way to go.

Consider an example. Both the Soviet Union and the United States invest a great deal in antiaircraft weapons. Now Soviet planners are not blessed with the education of American military management in business school efficiency. So what do they do? They have developed 12.7mm and 14.5mm antiaircraft *machine guns*, those weapons which the Afghan rebels are now using against the people who designed and built them. They also developed antiaircraft *guns*: 23mm cannon and 57mm guns. And they have developed many types of missile, the high altitude SAM-2, the medium SAM-3, and then the SAM-4, the long-range SAM-5, and later the short-range SAM-7 and SAM-9. Since then, newer missiles have replaced this lot, but there are even more different types. From the point of view of the Pentagon, what the Soviets have been doing is completely insane. They have all those different types of missiles and guns, with all those different spare parts needed for each, and with all the different training courses needed for the crews. It is a logistical nightmare! What the Pentagon seeks is to have one antiaircraft missile or at most two. The goal is to work out scientifically what is the best antiaircraft missile, to build it in one highly efficient factory so that only one set of spare parts is needed, one training center for crews—all for maximum efficiency. The only problem is that when you actually fly against a Soviet-style antiaircraft defense, if you fly very low, it hits you with the SAM-7s, even the machine guns, as well as cannon. If you fly at medium height, the SAM-4s, SAM-6s, and SAM-8s hit you. If you go as high as any aircraft can reach, the SAM-5s can still hit you. Whereas, against the optimum missile conceived of by the Americans, the Soviet pilot can underfly and overfly its height limits. Now when you go to McDonald's, you do not deliberately try to avoid eating hamburgers. But when you offer a missile to the enemy, he does not want to be shot down by it. Those of you with any experience in Vietnam will have encountered many instances of the misapplication of efficiency. The most famous case was the body count, itself a synthetic measure of success and failure in a war where one could not measure success and failure by the map. Unfortunately, the body count only measured the cost that the enemy was paying to win.

Let me make one final point. The most painful, perhaps: the culminating point of success. Think back to what the situation was before the United States became entangled in Vietnam: President John F. Kennedy, his beautiful wife, an economic boom, a man on the way to the moon, and nuclear superiority. The United States was way ahead of the Soviet Union in nuclear weapons. The Soviet Union was frantically trying to catch up. What was the state of the balance of power? Well, the United States was *really* on top. Now what does the logic of strategy imply one should do? One should do nothing—and try to spread rumors that one is actually rather weak. As it was, there was bound to be a reaction. Now what kind of reaction did we get? Well, for one thing, the French left the NATO alliance. Others did not leave. But when the United States became entangled in Vietnam, the allies stayed out, except for Australia and New Zealand (with token forces) and the South Koreans with two divisions. Our allies did not come in with us ostensibly because the United States was fighting a wrong war. Actually, they did not come in with us because they saw that the United States was so full of power that it was going all the way to Vietnam to look for enemies to fight. As a matter of fact, the United States was very active even in Laos. American power reached all the way to Laos because an excess of power was manifesting itself. Why do great nations fail to expand and rise without cease, as restaurant chains are slowly spreading over the planet? Why do they unfailingly reach a culminating point? Because they evoke resistance proportionate to their expansion.

My message is that if there had not been Vietnam, and the growth of American power had continued, there would have been a much stronger reaction later on. Not only France but other countries too would have left the NATO alliance. The Chinese would now be aligned with the Soviet Union rather than with the United States. The reason the United States has the Chinese on its side is because it became weak after the Vietnam War. Before the United States intervened in Vietnam, there was no sensing of the culminating point and therefore of the need for caution. Now what happens after Vietnam? What happens on the downslope? It is recovery. We should remember that we can overlearn anything, including the lessons of Vietnam. We found out that Laos is very far away from the United States. But we must realize that Nicaragua is much nearer to us.

Let me stop here to reiterate my initial argument. It is not the impact of Vietnam on American strategic thinking that I see, but rather the revival of American strategic thinking after Vietnam. We still make mistakes, but now we make them because of an honest stupidity, not because of a whole frame of mind that was programmed to fail.

---

QUESTION: You claim that the United States learned a lot from the Vietnam War. In looking at weapons design since then, we have the M-1 Abrams tank, we have the Bradley fighting vehicle, we have big jet fighters as opposed to small ones, and we have very expensive submarines and ships. Would you care to comment on that in light of the Vietnam experience?

ANSWER: Well, you have got me there. The impact of the post-Vietnam improvement was least on the engineering and design community. The Detroit command that designs tanks was completely uninfluenced by the war in Vietnam and went on doing the same thing that it has been doing since 1945, namely trying to design the world's best tank. Initially they always come up with truly the world's best tank. That is the tank which has everything, even a sauna. Then the budgeteers cut out some of the items, and we are left with three quarters of the world's best tank. Why do they not design cheaper tanks? The answer fundamentally is that it reflects the culture of the United States. What is the justification for sending four Americans in a tank that costs 1.8 million dollars versus sending them in a better tank that costs 2.2 million dollars when the somewhat more expensive tank is much safer?

I have no personal prejudice in favor of expensive weapons. But whenever I have gone through the steps of the analysis, more often than not the costly weapon makes sense. Do they overdo it? Of course they overdo it. But do they overdo it by much? Not so much. Should the United States be spending as much as twenty million dollars for an F-16 fighter plane, which, after all, is supposed to be a light-weight, low-cost aircraft? The answer is: no. But what is the cheapest fighter that could really do the job? Is it a one-million-dollar fighter? No. It is a six-million-dollar fighter.

QUESTION: How does strategic thinking apply to the situation in Nicaragua?

ANSWER: One has to make an assessment about the present and about the future. We look at the present and what do we see? Well, in Nicaragua there are leaders who like to pose before the cameras, who like to strike defiant poses. Whenever we refrain from criticizing them, Daniel Ortega and the Sandinista leaders react by provocations. If they are not photographed, filmed, and reported enough, they immediately invite Iran's minister of war to come to Managua, or they visit Moscow, to make sure that we criticize them again. These leaders are not interested in providing a sewage system for Managua or in developing the country. They want to pose in camouflage uniforms and black glasses. Well, what is the assessment to be made? I believe it is this: If the Sandinista leaders are left alone, they will not settle down to running a communist regime of the kind that we see in Bulgaria or Czechoslovakia. Instead, they will follow the Fidel Castro line and subordinate economic development and social progress and dedicate themselves to action on the international scene. They will want to start in Central America, but Castro has shown the way to global activism. The character of the Sandinista leaders is their destiny. And in character, the Sandinista leaders are not, in fact, revolutionary nation-builders. They are would-be actors on the world scene. Are they really dangerous? That is a judgment call. If the states around Nicaragua were strong, we would have nothing to worry about. But next to Nicaragua are Costa Rica, Honduras, and El Salvador. They are very fragile.

QUESTION: What do you consider the criterion of success in El Salvador?

ANSWER: The criterion of success in El Salvador from the point of view of the United States government was to avoid a guerrilla victory. There are only about six or seven thousand guerrillas in El Salvador now, and they are not terribly well equipped or well trained. Yet it appeared in 1981 that they might win. It seemed that they might march into San Salvador and raise the red flag. Initially, the criterion of success for the United States government was only to keep that from happening.

QUESTION: What thoughts or comments do you have with regard to the performance of the average American soldier in Vietnam?

ANSWER: Different units in different situations had exceptionally varied experiences in Vietnam. The headquarters over which General Westmoreland presided in Saigon, MACV was an enormous headquarters. There were enough officers there to administer every armed force in the world. Veterans of that bureaucracy did not perform well. They could not—when rank is devalued by numbers, officers have no chance to do well. As for units in the field, one could go to some units and conclude that the United States Army was on the verge of mutiny, and one could go to other units and see excellent soldiers in fine shape. Westmoreland was luckier than most observers because apparently he only encountered good units!

QUESTION: I would like to know your thoughts about the effect that public opinion had on the Vietnam War. When General Westmoreland was here, he seemed to think that public opinion in the United States played a major role in causing the American defeat in Vietnam. What do you think?

ANSWER: Well, that was a frightening aspect of the Vietnam War. Even if it had been the best of all possible wars, the most necessary of all possible wars, fought under the most clear-headed military leadership possible, it would still have been perfectly easy to *film* it so that it would seem a cruel, wanton, destructive, and purposeless war. One could have portrayed the United States Army in the Second World War in the same way. On television, one could show the United States Army in North Africa as raw troops facing the German Afrika Korps veterans. Kasserine Pass, bodies strewn over the countryside, TV correspondents asking: "Why are we dying in some nameless, godforsaken North African desert? I thought that the Japanese had attacked us. Why are we here to recapture the colonies of the British and the French?" It is very easy to do. Do I have an answer? No.

QUESTION: You mentioned that we might have overlearned a lesson from our experience in Vietnam. I was wondering what you meant. What exactly was the lesson and what danger does the overlearning present to the United States?

ANSWER: Well, the clearest lesson of the Vietnam War was: Do not go to faraway places for vague purposes. And the overlearning is: Do not go anywhere for any purpose. If that rule is followed, one can forget about strategy. You must throw yourself at the mercy of your enemy because in strategy you can never know "exactly what you are getting into." The secretary of defense in the Reagan administration, Casper Weinberger, a man of considerable political talent, enunciated his six-point doctrine on the preconditions of intervention. According to him, we must not go into combat unless we know *exactly* the situation and how it will evolve, and unless public support is guaranteed no matter what happens. It sounds right, but in strategy it does not work like that. If one waits for complete clarity, that comes only with death. If one insists on a situation of complete clarity, one must wait until Russian troops are marching down Pennsylvania Avenue toward the White House. One always has to act on the basis of a mixture of knowledge, fear, suspicion, and prejudice.

QUESTION: I have served six years as an enlisted man in the United States Navy, and from what I have read and from what I have seen, it seems to me that our military forces kind of overcontrol. In other words, all the officers always seem to be looking to the next level up to find out what to do instead of doing what they feel is militarily appropriate at that time.

ANSWER: I have written a book, *The Pentagon and the Art of War*, which deals with the problem you raise. One line of analysis in that book is a comparison of how many officers served at every level over time since 1945. What emerges is that there are too many senior officers. So they overcontrol downward, micromanage downward because their function is so subdivided. Too few officers are better than too many. If you are in a hurry to increase your military power, perhaps you should execute your generals! If there are not enough officers, they are forced to assume a great deal of responsibility. They are forced to concentrate on the most important things, leaving trivia aside. When they go into combat, they perform differently: they are used to responsibility, used to focusing on the most important thing, and not getting trapped by little things. But with an overofficered structure, each officer must have responsibilities if he is not to collide into the area of the next man. Suddenly it is war, and the officer is asked to take on the most awesome responsibility of all: life and death. Thus an underofficered structure, a little ragged at the edges, will cause some minor inefficiencies but will do much better in combat.

QUESTION: This might be an unfair question, but I would like to raise it, and if you want to pass on it that would certainly be understandable. I would like you to compare the relative strategic ability of the United States during the Second World War, at the operational level at any rate, or even at the level of grand strategy, to our present ability.

ANSWER: This raises a historical mystery. The prewar United States Army was very small and very provincial. It recruited officers overwhelmingly from the South and from a narrow social group. Those officers spent their lives in boring provincial posts. One would have expected that to yield ignorant and incapable officers. Remember, the United States Army was not in Germany or Korea; it had only Panama and the Philippines—both backwaters. One would have expected a narrow-minded, provincial officer corps. Then this country went to war. After a short time, it became apparent that the British did not have good generals. Historians cite Slim as an exception and Montgomery as only a possibility. The United States Army, by contrast, had many first-class division commanders, even first-class corps commanders. Beyond the famous names at the higher levels, there was an entire cohort of talented officers. For anybody who is interested in officer education and selection, this is a sobering lesson. The United States Army *should* have had bad officers. Reassuringly, it did have inferior junior officers during most of the Second World War, as compared with their German counterparts. But at the higher levels in the American military, the quality of leadership was inexplicably very high. So perhaps the way to generate good officers is to maintain a small, backwater, underbudgeted, forgotten army.

QUESTION: I am a little surprised that you did not say anything about the issue of how the South Vietnamese supported the war effort in their own country. From my point of view, their support would be more important than the support of public opinion or television reporters in the United States.

ANSWER: The support of the South Vietnamese was indeed the crucial factor, but only so long as the conflict was an internal war between the Vietcong and the Saigon government. But the fact is that after 1968, after the famous Tet Offensive, the Vietcong burnt themselves out, and the war became a north-south affair. With that, the South Vietnamese ceased to be protagonists and became the victims of the war. What happened during Tet in 1968 was this: the South Vietnamese population learned that if the Vietcong and the North Vietnamese ever won, life would be hell; and in the United States the public saw the television imagery, and many believed that the war was lost and that the South Vietnamese population did not oppose the Vietcong. The attitude of the South Vietnamese military was rather different. From their point of view, the war was their profession, not military service but the war itself. What was their attitude? Terrible. Were none of them any good? Some were.

QUESTION: How important do you think American policy errors concerning Vietnam were in a historical perspective?

ANSWER: Not very important. Even if we assume that everything had gone right and we had won, we would still have needed an American military presence in South Vietnam. At the moment the United States Army had left, the North Vietnamese would have marched south to start the war all over again. The fact is: Vietnam was too peripheral. Peripheral for us, not peripheral for Hanoi. The old men in Hanoi were bitterly determined to win, tenaciously determined to win. They liked the war. In fact, the moment the war ended in South Vietnam, they started another war in Cambodia, which continues to this day.

QUESTION: If common sense does not work in the realm of strategy, do you believe that the Reagan administration has a good chance of making it?

ANSWER: Touché! Very good. In strategy, if one acts by common sense, one usually fails. But that does not mean that one can succeed just by running to jump into the nearest river. The notion is to sense the moment of the paradoxical turn. Let us say that you develop a navigation device and you are now bombing quite accurately. You should be aware of the fact that the enemy is getting hurt and that he is striving to counter you. So do not rely upon your innovation for the future. You mass-produce the navigation device, but you must anticipate its decline in effectiveness and develop a backup as if it did not work.

QUESTION: You suggest that one way to strengthen the American armed forces would be to kill off some of the officers. Did not the Russians try to do that in 1938? And were not they beaten by the Finns?

ANSWER: It was not a seriously recommended action. The wonderful example is postrevolutionary France. The French guillotined their officers and then went on to conquer Europe. And, of course, now we have the case of Iran. One reason why the Iranians, in spite of terrific logistic difficulties barely alleviated by our few deliveries of missiles, are doing well is that they got rid of the shah's generals. Now in 1938, Stalin massacred his officer corps as part of the extensive purges carried out in the Soviet Union. Then he sent the Red Army to fight Finland, and it did very poorly. But I am not really sure how these things were connected. Did the purge of the Russian military help? No, it did not help. But would it really have made a big difference if Stalin had not killed off the officers? I am not sure. Why? Because in Finland the Russians were fighting a very different war from any war that their officers had ever prepared to fight.

QUESTION: Many people argue that Afghanistan is for the Soviet Union what Vietnam was for the United States. Would you agree with that analogy? Do you think that the Russians are fighting in Afghanistan better than Americans fought in Vietnam? What do you foresee developing in Afghanistan during the next ten years?

ANSWER: Well, we kept pouring troops into Vietnam. Not as many as Westmoreland wanted, but many. We were trying frantically to win by spring, or Christmas, or the next presidential election, or whatever. The Soviet Union, by contrast, has been running a leisurely imperial pacification in Afghanistan. The Russians have two hundred divisions on their books, but only five or six Soviet divisions are in Afghanistan. Their forces are not now frantically running around trying to pacify the territory, nor are they frantically trying to protect anybody. They are mostly sitting in some places and operating communications on the ring road between Herat, Kandahar, and Kabul. It is an imperial pacification. One keeps hearing that they want to leave. That is possible. But they are behaving as if their goal is to stay. They tell the Afghan rebels: "You fellows can run around in the mountains, but so long as you continue to resist, you will have to remain in the mountains. We control the towns and peaceful habitation." Meanwhile, the next generation of Afghans is being educated under Soviet tutelage. Soviet policy is not to try to kill all the resisters. Its aim is to wait for them to die out. That is how empires have always consolidated difficult provinces—by controlling the main places, by educating youth to accept imperial rule, and by outliving the resistance. Now admittedly, a strategy of this kind works much better against Danes or Portuguese than against Afghans, who quite like running around in the mountains. But the fact is that even Afghanistan is becoming urbanized.

At any rate, do not compare Soviet strategy in Afghanistan to United States conduct in Vietnam. Theirs is not the frantic attempt to win, but rather a relaxed imperial pacification whose main tool is massacre. There are no My Lai's* in Afghanistan, no

---

*On 16 March 1968, an American army platoon led by Lt. William Calley entered the village of My Lai near the northeast coast of South Vietnam. Although they met no resistance, Calley and his men moved through the

accidental killings, no cover-ups. In Afghanistan, massacre is done by order. No court-martials are in the offing. From the Soviet point of view, there are too many people in some areas of Afghanistan. The Soviets do not particularly want to kill them, they just want to expell them as refugees to Pakistan. But to do that, they have to kill quite a few, they have to bomb them a few times until they leave. That is how the Romans conquered England. It is not very nice. But in the past it has worked. As far as the Afghan war is concerned, television was never invented. There are no Afghan atrocities reported on television, not even in the United States, let alone in the Soviet Union.

QUESTION: When General Westmoreland was here, he said that the United States suffered no military defeats in Vietnam. And to me that sounded a lot like what the Germans said after the First World War: the stab in the back myth. Could you comment on what Westmoreland said?

ANSWER: Well, his statement implied that what the United States was doing militarily in Vietnam was germane to winning the war. Some of it was, much of it was not. Your statement identifies a danger, or what looked like a danger ten years ago. Of course, what Westmoreland really meant was only that the United States suffered no battlefield defeats. But the fact is that the United States was defeated in Vietnam. It had to leave the field of battle to the enemy. It had to abandon the country it said it would protect, the people it said it would protect. That is the most complete defeat. Irrelevant achievement earns no rewards in strategy.

QUESTION: To what extent have those who enthusiastically support the development of the Strategic Defense Initiative used the system of strategic thinking that you have delineated?

ANSWER: Those who advocate the SDI are a loose coalition. Some are technicians, some are thinking in purely military terms, some are thinking purely in political terms, and some think that the whole scheme is without military merit but that much will be gained by channeling resources into *new* military technology. Remember, when you take five extra billion dollars and give the money to the navy, it will use the money to perfect current systems to achieve a 3- or 4-percent improvement on the margin in aircraft

---

village and opened fire on the inhabitants. The incident was concealed for over a year, but eventually a military court found Calley guilty of the premeditated murder of at least twenty-two South Vietnamese civilians.

carriers and so on. If you give five billion dollars to any established force, it will use it for incremental improvements of 2 or 3 percent at the margin. SDI is different. Either the recipients will completely waste the money on some fantasy, or they will come up with major innovations. Finally, there are the true believers who really seek a total defense.

My own analysis is that if we have something that will encourage our Soviet friends to go into the bomber business and the cruise missile business instead of deploying ballistic missiles, the SDI can earn its keep. Ballistic missiles are the weapons that put us in a hair-trigger situation.

Who is doing the strategic analysis for the government? Not any one group but all of them. That is to say that the nation is considering the scheme. The only thing that distresses me about the SDI debate is the usual parade of Nobel Prize winners who keep going on television to say that this or that is impossible. Some should have a little disclaimer printed below their names. They are—some of them—the same people who said that the thermonuclear bomb was impossible. I am not saying that the thermonuclear bomb was nice, but they said that the thing was impossible. Such people are politicians, abusing their scientific credentials to issue purely political messages.

# THOMAS J. MCCORMICK

Thomas J. McCormick was born on 6 March 1933 in Cincinnati, Ohio. McCormick received a B.A. in 1955 and an M.A. in 1956 from the University of Cincinnati and a Ph.D. in 1961 from the University of Wisconsin. After studying American foreign relations under the guidance of Fred Harvey Harrington and William Appleman Williams, he won wide acclamation as a leading representative of the Wisconsin school of diplomatic history. During his distinguished academic career teaching courses on the history of American foreign policy, McCormick served as an assistant professor at Ohio University from 1960 to 1964, an associate professor at the University of Pittsburgh between 1964 and 1970, and a full professor at the University of Wisconsin from 1970 to the present.

Throughout his impressive scholarly career, McCormick has exhibited a strong interest in analyzing the relationship between the United States and East Asia. His best-known work on the topic appeared in book form in 1967 as *China Market: America's Quest for Informal Empire, 1893–1901*. Reflecting his commitment to the study of Oriental affairs, McCormick served between 1974 and 1977 on the United States-East Asian Committee of the Ford Foundation and the American Historical Association. He also gave the keynote address to the Japanese Association of American Studies in 1983 after delivering a series of lectures on American policy toward Asia at Japanese universities in Kyoto, Osaka, and Tokyo. In his latest contribution to the area of Asian studies, McCormick helped edit a collection published in 1985 as *America in Vietnam: A Documentary History*.

Beyond his work on Far Eastern problems, McCormick authored a number of seminal essays that helped shape the conceptual and methodological agenda of the entire field of American diplomatic history. He also joined with Lloyd Gardner and Walter LaFeber in writing a textbook to provide students with a sophisticated analytical framework for studying the history of American foreign policy. Their joint effort was published in 1973 as *Creation of the American Empire*. Finally, in 1989, McCormick published a significant reinterpretation of recent American foreign relations in a book entitled *America's Half-Century: United States Foreign Policy during the Cold War.*

Although his scholarship spans the entire field of American diplomatic history, McCormick remains especially fascinated by the relationship between the United States and East Asia. His next major research project will explore American policy toward the Pacific rim from 1945 to the present. Besides placing the Vietnam War in the context of the broader American effort to keep Asian countries functioning within the free-world trading system, McCormick will analyze the changing role of Pacific rim nations in the global economy since the end of the Vietnam War.

# FOUR

# AMERICAN HEGEMONY AND THE ROOTS OF THE VIETNAM WAR

## by Thomas J. McCormick

O n May Day, 1950, President Harry S. Truman began American involvement in the Vietnam War by pledging financial and moral support for the French effort to reimpose colonial rule in Indochina. Almost exactly a quarter of a century later, in April 1975, President Gerald Ford witnessed the denouement of that war with the fall of Saigon. In the intervening twenty-five years, the French were militarily defeated and relinquished their Southeast Asian empire; the American experiment of nation building in South Vietnam during the Eisenhower-Kennedy years ended ironically in an American-approved assassination of their own client, Ngo Dinh Diem; the attempt at a military solution through land and air escalation during the Johnson administration failed to produce the fabled light at the end of the tunnel; and the so-called Vietnamization of the Nixon era merely bought more time, at great cost in lives, without disguising the fact that defeat by any other name was still defeat.

Of late, a great deal of polemical literature has reexamined the Vietnam War. Most of it has been concerned with the conduct of the war between 1963 and 1973 and whether it could have been waged differently and with different results. Most of it, as well, has engaged in "scapegoating," and a number of groups have been charged with undermining the war effort. For example, the antiwar movement in the United States has been blamed for encouraging North Vietnam; the television media for inflaming public opinion at home; the American people and Congress for putting unnecessary restraints on the president; politicians for lacking the courage to give the military full rein to do their job; and the military itself for its careerism and strategic ineptitude. While many of these examinations are interesting, almost all of them operate in a vacuum and fail to ask (much less answer) the one crucial question. Why was America in Vietnam in the first place? What was it about this small, impoverished, peasant land halfway around the globe on the Asian continental rim that was worth a war? That was worth nearly 60,000 American lives; worth a polarized and confrontationist American society; worth the deterioration in America's trading position in the world; worth the decline of presidential legitimacy that set the stage for the Watergate affair and Nixon's resignation? In the face of such awesome costs, what was the nature of the national interests in Southeast Asia that produced the American commitment to wage war? What was it, moreover, that kept producing recommitment at times when it would have been feasible for the United States to cut bait rather than continue fishing, such as in 1954 after the Geneva Conference agreement, in 1963 after the assassination of Diem, or in 1968 after the Tet Offensive? Why were we in Vietnam and why did we persevere there for twenty-five years? Until we understand why America paid the terrible costs it did pay in Vietnam, it is impossible to speculate intelligently whether the national interests justified risking the payment of yet higher costs—almost certainly another half-million American troops, possibly a Chinese intervention and another Korean-style war, or even conceivably a limited nuclear war that might beget global Armageddon.

Why then were we in Vietnam? The answer to that deceptively simple question will forever defy discovery unless you first understand the role of *hegemony* in world affairs and the American determination to perform that role after World War II. Let us first explore the notion of hegemony. This examination is not tangential; it is the linchpin upon which any persuasive analysis of the Vietnam War must depend. And if you live to be a thousand, you will never understand American policy in Vietnam unless you first understand the concept of hegemony.

By hegemony, I mean most crudely that one single nation-state has paramount superiority over every other nation-state in terms of economic, military, and ideological power. It has the capacity to be the workshop, the banker, the policeman, the preacher, and the teacher of the world. Moreover, it has the will to use that vast, preponderant power to coerce or persuade most of the world to abide by its rules of international behavior, and to ostracize and isolate those who do not. Such periods of single-power hegemony have been rare in world history. Since Columbus's epic voyage five centuries ago, only perhaps the Dutch between 1650 and 1680, more certainly the British between 1815 and 1870, and the Americans clearly since 1945 have wielded such global influence. But when such instances of absolute hegemony have occurred, they have tended to coincide with long periods of sustained economic growth and relatively peaceful relations among at least the more developed nations.

There is a reason for the apparent coincidence. Hegemony seems to soften the contradiction between the two major features of modern history, capitalism and nationalism. In its purely economic form, capitalism is inherently internationalist in nature. In its constant effort to maximize profits, capital has always wished to be fluid and free, able to go wherever the return was greatest, whatever the distance to be traveled and whatever the boundaries to be crossed. Relatedly, in its drive to enlarge the universe of profit-making opportunities, capital has always sought to bring into the world market the subsistence economies of the Americas, Africa, and Southeast Asia and the quasi-feudal empires of the Ottomans, the Chinese, and the Russians. On the other hand, the modern nation-state and its handmaiden, nationalism, have tended toward economic self-sufficiency rather than economic interdependence. Wedded to the defense of specific territory and to the sustenance of its own citizens, an individual nation-state leaned toward nationalism in its tariff policies, farm programs, military spending, and the like. Even its geographic expansion into less developed areas tended to take the form of colonialism, that is, an economic monopoly that integrated third-world areas only into a given country's national market rather than into a free-world market generally. In short, nationalism put barriers in the way of capitalism's effort to make itself more international and therefore more profitable. Thus economic internationalism was thwarted by political nationalism.

Single-power hegemony can partially overcome that contradiction. By definition, every hegemonic power historically has had a self-interest in promoting internationalism so that its capital could successfully compete anywhere and everywhere: hence the Dutch push for freedom of the seas, the British push for free trade, and the American push for a free world. Moreover, the

hegemonic power has had the strength to enforce its will on others
—to require them to sublimate their tendencies toward nationalism
and self-sufficiency and play by the rules of a free world, where
capital, goods, services, technology, advertising, and ideology are
free to move across national boundaries with minimal restrictions.
Great Britain performed that hegemonic function in the nineteenth
century between the Napoleonic Wars and the Franco-Prussian
War. And by extension, the long-term decline of British hegemony—and the scramble to take its place by Germany, the United
States, and Japan—may arguably have been at the root of both
world wars and the Great Depression in this century.

World War II ended that scramble and firmly established
the United States at Britain's hegemonic successor. Gore Vidal put
it well in his novel *Washington, D.C.*, where he described the situation at the moment of President Roosevelt's death in 1945:

> The . . . ravaged old President . . . even as he was dying, [contin-
> ued] to pursue the high business of reassembling the fragments of
> broken empires into a new pattern with himself at center, proud
> creator of the new imperium. Now, though he was gone, the work
> remained. The United States was master of the earth. No England,
> no France, no Germany, no Japan . . . left to dispute the Repub-
> lic's will; only the mysterious Soviet would survive to act as other
> balance in the scale of power.

Vidal is not off the mark. America emerged from World War II as
the dominant power par excellence led by a foreign policy elite of
New Deal liberals and business internationalists determined to use
that power to reconstruct the world system after ten years of a terrible depression and six years of a terrible war; to replace the Pax
Britannica of the nineteenth century with the Pax Americana of the
twentieth century; to use America's economic power to mold a
world system of free trade and free seas and free currency convert-
ibility; to use its military power as world policeman to give the
world system a sense of security against internal revolutions or external challenges; and to use its ideological power to command deference to and acceptance of its dominant values and ideas.

Between 1945 and 1950, the United States used its new hegemonic position to attempt the reconstruction of European capitalism through the Marshall Plan and of Japanese capitalism
through the lesser-known Dodge Plan. Its monopoly of the atomic
bomb served as a military shield to force much of the world to look
to it for protection. Policymakers in Washington also manipulated
American public opinion to prevent any revival of protectionism

and isolationism and to ensure bipartisan support for foreign aid and internationalism. But by early 1950, three crises interacted in a volatile way to threaten this Pax Americana before it ever got off the ground, and the response of the American foreign policy elite to that triple crisis was to transform Vietnam and Indochina from a place of marginal importance for the national interest to one of centrality.

One part of the crisis was the deterioration in world capitalism that raised the specter of a slide back into the prewar depression. In Asia, the Dodge Plan for Japan proved a calamity, and by early 1950 that country's economy was on the brink of national bankruptcy. In Europe, midpoint projections on the Marshall Plan produced gloomy predictions that it was going to prove both too little and too short-term. In each instance, the causes were similar. Both European and Japanese production did begin to revive, but viable markets for that production remained stagnant. As George Frost Kennan put it in August 1949, "It is one thing to produce; it is another thing to sell." That is, European and Japanese domestic consumption suffered from austerity-imposed low wages, and the foreign markets necessary to take up the slack did not materialize. Why not? The largest capitalist market (the United States) was partially restricted by congressional protectionism; the socialist market (the Soviet bloc) was obstructed by the developing Cold War; and the third-world periphery (including Southeast Asia) had not been sufficiently revived and reintegrated as suppliers of food and raw materials and as consumers of finished products. Clearly, unless Europe and Japan could find viable markets and cheap raw materials to reduce their own manufacturing costs, they could not continue indefinitely to sustain their enormous trade deficit with the United States. They might be forced to defy American hegemonic rules and resort to the customs duties, currency restrictions, and capital controls that had characterized foreign economic policies in the Great Depression and, perhaps, had caused World War II.

Two other key factors exacerbated this crisis in postwar capitalism, and both involved the Soviet Union. The first was the Russian explosion of a nuclear test device in late 1949, which unexpectedly ended America's monopoly of the atomic bomb. While most American leaders, interestingly, did not fear the military implications of this event, they did fear its political and psychological implications. They were concerned that Europe and Japan might question the credibility of America's military shield and wonder whether the United States would risk atomic attack on its homeland in order to defend them against possible Russian intimidation. In other words, American leaders feared the atomic bomb less than they feared atomic diplomacy; they feared that Europe and Japan might waver in their deference to American hegemony and be tempted to play the Russian card—to work out some economic and political accommodation with the Soviets that might violate the American rules of economic internationalism and collective security.

The second exacerbating factor was the final triumph of Mao Zedong and the Communist Party in the Chinese Civil War and the signing of a Sino-Soviet Pact in February 1950. That development seemed to signal China's partial withdrawal from the capitalist world system and raised further concern that the Asian rimlands of Korea, Taiwan, and Southeast Asia would soon emulate that withdrawal. Given Japan's near bankruptcy and its historical economic dependence on Northeast Asia and Southeast Asia, given Britain's economic stake in Hong Kong, Singapore, Malaya, and India, there was real fear in Washington that the Japanese and/ or the British might be tempted to work out an economic and political accommodation with the Sino-Soviet bloc that again would undermine the free-world rules of economic internationalism.

Consider what all this meant: for five years, American elites had attempted to use their hegemonic power and position to effect the recovery of the European and Japanese industrial machines and to restore world trade to predepression levels and at the same time isolate ("contain") the Soviet bloc, which declined to defer to American hegemony and accept American rules of the game. Now, all that seemed terribly jeopardized. Japan's economic recovery was in a shambles and Europe's was disappointing; both were running an unmanageable trade deficit with the United States. Most of Eurasia, from the Elbe to the Amur, had partially withdrawn from the world economy. The Asian rimlands seemed destined to follow soon, and there was fear that much of the third world might not be far behind. Moreover, America's atomic diplomacy and the credibility of its military shield appeared much in doubt. In the eyes of American leaders, 1950 seemed frighteningly like 1930, with strong centrifugal tendencies pushing nation-states to revert to their inherent nationalist tendencies. This nationalist impulse tempted them to protect their own economies through state regulation of trade and investment or to reach accommodation with the Soviet Union and China to ease their own deficit/ debtor dilemmas. In other words, American hegemony was facing its first and severest postwar test, and if that hegemony could not be maintained, there were serious questions in the minds of American elites as to whether the capitalist world economy and the American free-enterprise system could survive and prosper.

The response of American leaders was two-fold. First, they chose to militarize the Cold War, i.e., they decided to build the H-bomb, quadruple the military budget, replace foreign economic aid with military aid, transform NATO from a political alliance to a military one, and rearm Germany and perhaps Japan. All this would magnify the credibility of American military protection for our allies and would be easier to sell in the name of national security and anticommunism to the public and Congress at home. Second, they chose to make a concerted effort to develop third-world extractive economies and integrate them into the industrial economies of Europe and Japan in order to provide the markets and cheap raw materials necessary for the full and permanent recovery of the industrial core. Perpetuating the unequal world division of labor, American leaders sought not to develop the third world industrially. They aimed merely to raise the productivity and lower the costs of third-world raw materials and foodstuffs. This is known as limited or dependent development.

These two new trends in the Cold War—militarization and third-world orientation—came to be focused on the Asian rimlands in the 1950s and the early 1960s. This focus reflected both American fear and American hope. The fear was that Korea, Taiwan, and Vietnam—already enveloped in revolutionary situations—would quickly gravitate into a Chinese sphere of influence, and that the potential loss of Northeast Asia and Southeast Asia as Japanese markets and raw material sources would mean the gradual shift of Japan from the free-world trading system to an Asian state trading bloc. The result would be the Asian Co-Prosperity Sphere* that the United States had fought World War II to avoid. The hope, reflected in National Security Council Memorandum 48/2, was that bold action could reverse these trends. American leaders hoped that the Asian rimlands could yet be politically stabilized, economically developed, and made independent of a Chinese sphere; that a formal peace treaty with Japan could be effected as the prelude to a peaceful economic reintegration of the rimlands into the Japanese "workshop" economy; that lost areas in Northeast Asia (Korea and Manchuria) might yet be "liberated" and re-

---

*In 1938 the Japanese announced that they would establish a vast regional economic bloc whose doors would be closed against Western trade and investment. Japanese business interests would enjoy special commercial and financial privileges in this so-called Greater East Asia Co-Prosperity Sphere.

stored to the world system; and that ultimately, the successful integration of Japan and the Asian rimlands might not only save the Japanese industrial core but perhaps eventually wean China away from the Soviet Union and back down the capitalist road.

American government documents of the 1950s and early 1960s abound with references to this fear and this hope. For example, the Council of Economic Advisers to the President stated that

> The crux of Japan's recovery problem is her foreign trade . . . With colonies lost, and conditions chaotic in Northeast Asia, Japan is . . . looking to unsettled Southeast Asia as a supplementary source of food and other imports and a probable major market for fabricated products.

The Department of State declared that

> cooperation of Southeast Asia nations may become absolutely essential if Japan is to be kept from falling into Soviet arms as the result of economic opportunities in Northeast Asia

and the Department of Defense stated that

> continuing, or even maintaining Japan's economic recovery will depend upon keeping communism out of Southeast Asia, promoting economic recovery there and in further developing these countries as the principal trading areas for Japan.

The National Security Council stated that

> The fall of Southeast Asia would underline the apparent economic advantages to Japan of association with the communist-dominant sphere. Exclusion of Japan from trade with Southeast Asia would seriously affect the Japanese economy. . . . In the long run, the loss of Southeast Asia, especially Malaya and Indonesia, could result in such economic and political pressures in Japan as to make it extremely difficult to prevent Japan's eventual accommodation to the soviet bloc.

and the Joint Chiefs of Staff said that

> [Japan's cooperation with the U.S.] will be significantly affected by her ability to retain access to her historic markets and sources of food and raw materials in Southeast Asia. Viewed in this context, U.S. objectives with respect to Southeast Asia and U.S. objectives with respect to Japan would appear to be inseparably related. . . . The loss of Southeast Asia to the Western World would almost inevitably force Japan into an eventual accommodation with the Communist-controlled areas in Asia.

What all this means is obvious. The original American commitment in Vietnam in 1950 was made as part of a policy of regionalism designed to integrate Japan and Southeast Asia in ways that would promote and sustain Japanese economic recovery and its place in the world trading system. And that motivation remained the principal motivation for American involvement in Vietnam until the mid-1960s, when changing circumstances made it easier for Japan to enter the American market, develop its own home market, and be less dependent on Southeast Asia although even then, the motivation remained very important for American policymakers. Indeed, it was amplified by a further consideration, the increasing Japanese dependence on Persian Gulf oil and the strategic importance of Southeast Asia in protecting the trade routes traveled by Japan-bound oil tankers.

There are three important corollary observations that follow from this "Japanese connection" interpretation of the Vietnam War. First, and most obviously, the United States did not act out of direct and immediate interest of its own; its economic and security interests in Southeast Asia were marginal. But for Japan (and to a lesser extent, for Europe), the interests were absolutely vital. And it is for them that the United States acted. From the viewpoint of American elites, this was, after all, the essence of hegemony; if one wishes to reap the rewards of power—prestige and profits—then one must bear the burdens of power. In the case of Vietnam, the burden was primarily political and military, although the objective of development and integration was economic. As one State Department official put it:

> The first perquisite to economic recovery in Asia is not increased production and exports . . . but effective solutions for fundamental political and military conflicts which are stifling production and trade. Given those political and military solutions, economic recovery could be attained rapidly, . . . and with relatively little capital expenditure.

Economic development required political stability, and there could be no political stability until there was military pacification.

The second corollary to the "Japan connection" thesis is that the United States took the domino theory quite seriously and felt that Japan was the ultimate domino. It is only in this conceptual framework that Vietnam matters. Otherwise, Vietnam is merely small, poor, and unimportant; certainly, this becomes evident when it is compared with a major Southeast Asian country like Indonesia with a population of over one hundred million and raw materials vast in quantity and in variety. But Vietnam *was* the most volatile country in Southeast Asia; it was the locus of a radical revolution and a nationalist, anticolonial war, and as such, it primed the sensitive feelings of a region historically hostile to Western colonialism, racism, and economic exploitation. In short, there was real fear that a successful, anti-Western, anticapitalist revolution in Vietnam might spark a Pan-Asian movement that might lead all of Indochina to reject the capitalist world system and gravitate to China. This in turn might induce the major archipelagos of Indonesia and the Philippines to follow suit, and ultimately, Japan itself. The end result would be a Pan-Asian bloc integrating China, Japan, and Southeast Asia and limiting the economic access essential for American and European capitalism. The prospect of Asia for Asians was seen as a new version of the so-called yellow peril.

The final thesis corollary of the "Japanese connection" is that the American commitment in Vietnam involved making a choice that valued Japanese industrial recovery over the political and economic aspirations of Southeast Asian nationalism. American policymakers were not ignorant or uninformed. They understood that their pro-Japanese policy of economic regionalism would be highly unpopular in Southeast Asia, even among anticommunists. They were aware of the strong residue of hostility toward Japan and its wartime occupation, and they realized that Southeast Asia was unwilling to play a subordinate, unequal role in the world economy at the expense of developmental dreams. American policymakers saw the likelihood that the United States would be suspected of reviving Western economic imperialism in the name of anticommunism. It thus came as no surprise when Southeast Asian commentators gave voice to their opposition to American plans. As the moderate *Manila Times* put it:

> Why should the Philippine republic agree to a deal under which the Japanese will profit and prosper and the Philippines will remain on the old colonial basis of providing basic raw materials to a former enemy in exchange for the modern equivalent of glass beads, brass rings and hand mirrors. Especially when the Philippines can make its own.

Yet understanding all that, American policymakers still set aside their own anticolonialism, their expressed sympathy for third-world nationalism, and pressed on with their policy. For in their scheme of things, anticolonialism was a minor good compared to the major good of reviving productivity in industrial core countries like Japan. The most that American leaders could and would do was attempt to soften the impact of their choice by stressing nation building and Vietnamization in the 1950s and resorting only to direct American military involvement in the 1960s.

There were, as I noted previously, at least three times when American policy might have been reconsidered: in 1954 after the French defeat; in 1963 after Diem's death; and in 1968 after Tet. But each time, basic policy was reconfirmed or only partly modified. In part, this reflected the most obvious fact that American goals were still not realized and still had to be pursued. Southeast Asia was still not pacified, stabilized, developed, and integrated wholly into the Japanese economy. But other considerations also came to the fore to reinforce that central tendency. For example, in 1954, the United States could have accepted the Geneva Accords and let nature take its course, but it decided not to do so. Instead, the United States launched an attempt to build an autonomous South Vietnam nation under Ngo Dinh Diem. Part of the reason lay in concern for American credibility. Even during the French phase of the fighting from 1950 to 1954, the United States made clear to its allies that it considered Southeast Asia to be its sphere of responsibility, and the French defeat did not change that crucial fact. An American commitment had been made in Indochina as a function of American hegemony, and failure to fulfill that commitment, it was feared, might erode the very credibility on which that hegemony ultimately rested. This was especially true in Asia in the mid-1950s. The Japanese Security Treaty, the Southeast Asian Treaty Organization, the Australian-New Zealand-U.S. pact—all had created a multitude of new, formal political-military commitments that might be shaken in their infancy by an American decision to back out of Indochina. As one secretary of state was fond of noting, the United States had treaty commitments to forty-two nations in the world system, and failure to fulfill one treaty jeopardized all. This is a classic assessment of the perils of hegemony and playing world policeman.

After Diem's death in 1963, another factor powerfully reinforced the Japanese variable and the decision not only to stay in Vietnam but also to escalate American involvement. That was the American desire to use Vietnam as an example, to demonstrate that revolutionary violence was not a tolerable way of effecting social change in the world system. Keep in mind the context: Cuba under Fidel Castro had pulled off a successful, radical, anti-American revolution in America's traditional Caribbean sphere of influence; the Congo crisis heralded the awakening of a revolutionary independence movement in Africa; and the Soviet Union pledged its support for wars of national liberation, even those led by bourgeois noncommunists. Cuba especially rankled, for if the United States could not maintain regional hegemony in its own so-called backyard, could it maintain any serious pretense to global hegemony? Sustaining the commitment in Vietnam was one way to do so, but only if the commitment produced victory, and hence the decision to escalate direct American military involvement. (I might digressively add here that Cuba played a further role in the escalation decision. If the Bay of Pigs in 1961* had humiliated American leaders, then the Cuban missile crisis of 1962† elated them. As Secretary of State Rusk boasted, the United States had gone "eyeball to eyeball" with the Soviet Union in a nuclear game of chicken, and the "other guy [had] blinked." The result was a kind of macho giddiness that made American officials more in-clined to military adventurism.)

Finally, after the Tet Offensive in 1968, another factor inter-vened to sustain America's longest war. By that juncture, most members of the inner circle of power in the United States had de-termined that the war had become counterproductive. They con-cluded that they had underestimated the will of their adversary and that American fighting morale was too low to be effectively revived. Moreover, wartime inflation was undermining American competitiveness in world markets, and the campus antiwar move-ment threatened to alienate permanently a whole generation vital to corporate America as engineers, lawyers, managers, and profes-sionals. Finally, our European and Japanese allies felt that our myo-pia about Vietnam had led us to neglect our other responsibilities in the world system. In short, many policymakers reasoned that the Vietnam War was beginning to undermine the very hegemony it was supposed to confirm. Indeed, on the basis of those consid-erations, the elite Senior Advisory Group on Vietnam—sometimes known as The Wisemen—advised President Johnson in early 1968 to cut his losses and get out. And many of these same people told Richard M. Nixon the same thing when he assumed the presidency

---

*After leading a successful revolution in 1959, Fidel Castro established a communist regime in Cuba. In 1961, a group of CIA-trained Cuban dissi-dents were transported to Cuba on American ships and waded ashore at the Bay of Pigs. But their attempt to inspire an armed insurrection against Castro ended in failure.

†A confrontation between the United States and the Soviet Union occurred in 1962 when American spy planes discovered Russian missile installations in Cuba. President John F. Kennedy pressured Premier Nikita S. Khrush-chev into withdrawing the Soviet missiles from Cuba.

a year later. And he believed them, acknowledging privately that he knew we could not win the war. And yet the war did not end. Air bombings increased, the land war expanded into Cambodia, and another twenty-six thousand Americans were killed in action. There was only one reason for this determination: no occupant of the Oval Office was willing to go into history books as the first American president to lose a war. Johnson chose not to run for reelection rather than endure that fate, and Nixon put Indochina through the meatgrinder of Vietnamization for four years in order to obscure and escape that fate.

In summary, the United States emerged from World War II with both the power and the will to function as the hegemonic leader in the capitalist world system: its banker, its policeman, its ideologue. The American commitment in Vietnam was made as an exercise of that hegemonic function: to prevent Southeast Asia from opting out of the world system and thus insuring the viability of Japanese economic recovery by regional integration with Asian rimlands and holding out the long-term possibility of enticing China back into the world system. That commitment, in turn, was periodically reinforced by a desire to preserve the credibility that, by definition, was an integral part of hegemony. Vietnam served as a test case to demonstrate to the third world that violent social change and withdrawal from the system were not acceptable and would not work. America stayed in Vietnam because of the desire to save face by successive chief executives—presidents not only of the United States, but leaders of the free world (i.e., the world system)—an office we could call the imperial presidency.

In an obvious sense, American policy failed. The war was lost and Vietnam fell, followed by Laos and Cambodia; revolution as a vehicle of social change was not deterred and indeed continued to unfold with increasing rapidity in Central America, the Persian Gulf, and sub-Saharan Africa; and American hegemony did come to be questioned, even by its closest allies (although the questioning was less about the extent of American power than the rationality of its application). On the other hand, the goal of keeping Asia in the world trading system has, for the moment, apparently been realized. Japanese economic recovery has been stunning, even unsettlingly so; the Asian rimlands abound with seemingly capitalist showplaces in South Korea, Taiwan, Singapore, and Hong Kong; the major dominoes in Southeast Asia, Indonesia and the Philippines, did not fall—at least not yet, and China itself has been estranged from the Soviet Union and opted for a partial return to the capitalist system. From that perspective, one could argue that Vietnam was a partial vindication of American hegemony. But the final determinant of whether Vietnam was a victory or a disaster depends largely on what lessons were learned from Vietnam and how those lessons affected (and affect) American policy since Vietnam. The crucial question is: Did Vietnam herald a decline in America's hegemonic position in the world system and the need to accommodate to that change? Or did Vietnam dramatize a need for stronger commitments and a more militarized policy to regain that hegemonic position?

Taken on balance, the Indochina war helped produce the very thing it sought to avoid—an erosion of American hegemony and waning legitimacy of its global suzerainty. The political evidence is obvious in the increasing multipolarity of the world system: the emergence of Japan and Germany as major capitalist rivals and potential power centers; the fracturing of the Soviet bloc witnessed by the Sino-Soviet split, the Polish Solidarity movement, and Eastern European arrangements with Western banks and multinationals; and the rise of forces like Islamic fundamentalism that simply do not conform to traditional Cold War categories. Just as obvious is the economic evidence: the OPEC oil shocks; the breakdown of the postwar international monetary system; the decline in American industrial productivity and the development of an enormous American trade deficit; the appearance of newly industrialized countries in a select portion of the third world as multinationals move their branch plants abroad in search of lower costs and higher profits; and the revival of protectionist sentiment, even in an America that for forty years had preached that the world ought to be free rather than restricted.

These centrifugal tendencies in the world system have produced an intense debate within the American foreign policy elite about American hegemony: How much has it declined in the aftermath of Vietnam; how much can be restored; and by what means? That debate has been active now for a decade, first surfacing in the Carter administration in the duel between the Cyrus Vance faction and the Zbigniew Brzezinski faction, and more currently, in the Robert McNamara-McGeorge Bundy critique of Reagan's Strategic Defense Initiative, or Star Wars, program. One polemicist has called it the debate between "the traders" and "the Prussians." The former, somewhat more representative of an older "Yankee" eastern elite, have tended to be more sanguine about the decline of American hegemony and are inclined to accept it as an inevitable fact of life (empires rise and empires fall: even the American). This faction has argued that Vietnam demonstrated the inefficacy of military solutions and the need to accept limits on America's role as world policeman and that Vietnam undermined American moral leadership by making the United States the perpetrator of what much of the world saw as a racist, colonial war. Only a vigorous human rights diplomacy, the "traders" reasoned, could restore America's moral legitimacy as world leader. Reindustrialization could revive American productivity and correct America's trade deficit. This side of the debate argued that we could learn to live with and profit from third-world revolutions—whether they called themselves African socialists, or Arabian socialists, or Marxist-Leninists, none could deliver their material promises to their subjects without coming to the West, hat in hand, for capital and technology.

The other side of the debate, the "Prussians," somewhat more representative of a new elite, have been ill-disposed to accept the loss of American hegemony; much like during the 1950 crisis, they have opted to remilitarize the Cold War as a solution. They have argued that hegemony should be rebuilt on the basis of an enlarged and modernized military shield, so that the United States alone can provide the system with protection, for which it receives special consideration. This group argues that human rights diplomacy is ineffective and that deference based on fear is more real than deference based on sentimental or moral considerations. The "Prussians" oppose reindustrializing weak and noncompetitive industries as a waste of resources, but advocate the creation of whole new industries through the technological spin-off of the Star Wars project as the way to restore American economic supremacy over Japan, Germany, and Russia. Third-world revolutions might be profitable, in their view, but giving them free rein would negate the very policeman function that would be the given reason for America's refurbished and remilitarized hegemony.

In a sense, the debate is a replay of the 1950 debate that produced the first militarization of the Cold War. Or of earlier and similar debates in British society a century ago. Or of yet more ancient debates in Rome. Is the American empire falling or merely regrouping for another ascent to the summit? And if it is falling, will it go out with a bang or a whimper—or some more gracious way?

---

QUESTION: Do you not find it extremely ironic, in terms of your view as to what we were doing in Vietnam, that we fought the Japanese in World War II to prevent them from creating an

Asian Co-Prosperity Sphere, and then we went to all this trouble to reinstitute what we had tried to prevent?

ANSWER: It is at one level. It is seemingly ironic because, indeed, as you suggest, it looks like we were recreating the very thing that we had fought to avoid in World War II. But there really is a difference that I must make clear, and that is in World War II the real fear was, of course, that if Japan by unilateral military force established its own Asian sphere it would have been fine for Japan. But American leaders anticipated that it would be an autarkic, self-contained Asian sphere which would carry on only managed trade relations with the West. Consequently, access to Asia for American capital, American technology, and American goods would be more limited. It was not the region that America's leaders opposed, it was the fact that they thought the region would opt out of the world system and be closed to American capital and American commodities. In the later Vietnam case, the economic regionalism would serve Japan in the first instance, but we assumed that any concessions we might win for the Japanese ultimately down the pike would be useful to us as well. So the one difference—doing it under American aegis—in the Vietnam era is that we are insuring that the area will not only be open for Japan but that it will also be open for the United States. Indeed, as it happened, the United States did develop over time an interesting sort of triangular trade relationship involving Japan, Southeast Asia, and the United States that eventually gave this country something of a stake in the entire region.

QUESTION: As I remember World War II, one of the complaints the Japanese had against the United States was that we had imposed certain embargos on the shipment of oil and steel and other things to Japan. But it seems to me completely ridiculous to think that the Japanese could not and would not have interacted with the United States and the rest of the world even if they did carve out a portion of Asia for themselves.

ANSWER: I am not suggesting that a Japanese-dominated Asia would have ceased all economic intercourse with the United States and Europe. But the creation of a Greater East Asian Co-Prosperity Sphere would have sharply reduced the volume and profitability of East-West trade. One of the major goals of Japan's Pan-Asianism was to make the region nearly autarkic—nearly self-contained and self-sufficient. Instead of buying their oil, coal, timber, iron ore, cotton, and various foodstuffs from this country, the Japanese sought to develop alternative sources in China, Northeast

Asia, and Southeast Asia. Moreover, they sought to establish a system of direct barter so that they could exchange their surplus manufactured goods for those primary commodities. Trade in Asia would become mainly intraregional rather than international. The end result would be a serious diminution of participation in the world economy by Japan, China, and the rest of Asia.

QUESTION: What similarities do you see between the United States' policies in Vietnam and in Central America? Do you see us getting into the same situation in Central America five or ten years down the road that we did in Vietnam?

ANSWER: That is a difficult question. I think, in the first place, there are some similarities. For example, the role of credibility is not insignificant. If the Russians can keep order in their house, i.e., in Afghanistan, but if we cannot keep order in our "backyard," in the Caribbean, can American credibility be taken seriously elsewhere in the world? So even if Central America per se is of marginal importance, and even if American leaders no longer take the domino theory seriously and assume that if Nicaragua falls, Mexico City goes the day after tomorrow and Brownsville the day after, the notion of credibility does, I think, matter to them. Again, as I have suggested, policymakers currently in power advocate the remilitarization of American foreign policy and stress the American policeman role. This is the only reason for an industrial country to defer to us any longer. We have a comparative advantage in two things: military and agricultural products. Unless the world system can look to the United States for military muscle, there is no commanding logic in accepting American leadership. So in that sense, I think there are some similarities.

I would hesitate to say where it might lead; there are too many variables. One of the variables that is different now, and one of the reasons why Vietnam was very important is the fact that Vietnam put a dent in the public consensus supporting the idea that the United States should play the role of global policeman. From World War II onward, American leaders made an implied social contract with the American public that said we can play world policeman, and we can get all the material and psychic rewards that go with playing that role, and we can do it without making a lot of sacrifices. World War II itself was fought as a kind of limited war; it employed a mobilization strategy and a military strategy that maximized economic rewards while it minimized battlefield casualty lists. Even the way the United States ended World War II by dropping the atomic bomb was a way of saying to the American people: "You can play policeman after the war is over and it will not cost you a thing. We have the bomb, have an atomic monopoly, and we can play world policeman on the cheap." I think that by and large most folks bought into this idea. But Vietnam dented that belief. Vietnam may not have destroyed it, for it has great residual power. There is a great psychic comfort in the notion that the United States can be number one. Nonetheless, I think Vietnam dented the conviction that the United States really could be world policeman and not pay some costs for assuming that task. So I think folks are a little more leery of shouldering that burden. By folks, I do not necessarily mean the antiwar protest movement. Rather, I mean what Nixon called the silent majority. Americans began to feel the heavy price that they paid in terms of inflation, in terms of the prospect of higher taxes, in terms of the loss of people they loved. The American people have not forgotten these things, and the mere fact that you are here indicates that amnesia has not occurred. There is a collective memory about Vietnam that does impose some restraints and brakes upon what American policymakers might or might not do in the future. So even if they thought that they had the power to effect a militarized solution in Central America, they might be inhibited by the post-Vietnam public opinion.

So I think their preference is a kind of insider-outsider strategy where they try to work through inside groups, i.e., the Contras, and use economic, diplomatic, and military pressures from without to create an unstable environment in Nicaragua so that the Sandinistas, over time, will not be able to deliver on their material promises to the people supporting them. American leaders hope to impose harsh penalties so that the Sandinista regime will unravel from within. That is their real goal. I do not think they want to send American troops to Nicaragua if they can avoid it.

QUESTION: I want to raise three points that conflict with the main reason you give for the American involvement in Southeast Asia. The first point is that Japan itself was devastated after the Second World War, and I do not think it was really that much concerned about markets in Southeast Asia. Secondly, I think that the reason the United States intervened in Vietnam was more to preserve the honor of the French after their defeat in World War II at the hands of Germany. Thirdly, the real crucial state you mentioned in Southeast Asia was Indonesia, and the United States let Sukarno's Indonesia go down the socialist path into the Sino-Soviet bloc.

ANSWER: I first address the question whether or not the Japanese were interested in Southeast Asia. Japan is a classic export-or-die economy. It is an economy that, unlike our own, is very deficient in food and raw materials and needs to export to pay for the import of those things. Since the Meiji Restoration of the late nineteenth century,* the Japanese have never been uninterested in opening up avenues of trade in Asia. Their secondary area of interest was Northeast Asia, particularly Korea and Manchuria, but commerical intercourse with that region was not politically feasible for them after World War II. Their optimal area for economic penetration was China, and the United States feared that Japan might take that route. Given the dearth of options, the Japanese were very, very interested in Southeast Asia. Japanese documents confirm this point. They show that the Japanese were extraordinarily excited about economic prospects in Southeast Asia. Even before the Korean War bailed out the Japanese economy with American military subcontracts, the Japanese were interested in Southeast Asia, and as soon as the Korean War ended, they directed their attention to Southeast Asia again.

As to France, I think you can make a case that in the early postwar period there was some American concern. I do not think we worried about French honor. But I do think we cared about whether or not the French would play their proper role in the Marshall Plan for European economic recovery. We hoped that the French would not block the rearming of Germany. We wanted the French to accept EDC—the European Defense Community.† Thus we were susceptible to French political blackmail that if we did not help out in Vietnam, the French polity might move to the left or even toward the communists. So there was, I fully acknowledge, great concern about France, particularly during the period between 1946 and 1950. But the Japanese variable already by 1950 had outstripped any early concerns for the French variable; and, of course, the latter was dead by 1954 when the French pulled out of Vietnam after the Geneva Accords.

---

*The state played a major role in promoting industrial development in Japan during the late nineteenth century. The so-called Meiji Restoration was prompted by a desire on the part of the Japanese to use Western technology to defend themselves against Western imperialism.

†Favoring the remilitarization of Germany in 1952, the United States supported a proposal for the creation of a European Defense Community. The idea was to integrate Germany into a multilateral European military force. The French vetoed the scheme in 1954, but they ultimately bowed to Anglo-American pressure and agreed to allow Germany to participate in the North Atlantic Treaty Organization.

As to Indonesia, I would dispute that we let Indonesia and Sukarno go down the socialist road. American policymakers were enormously unhappy with what was going on there, and they may have encouraged the army coup that overthrew the left-leaning regime in Indonesia. The first doves in the American establishment were those who said: "Look, Indonesia has been saved. That was the big one we were concerned about. But Sukarno is gone, and the good guys are in power, and they are marching to a tune that we can accept. So let's cool it in Vietnam and seek some form of political disengagement." But while some American leaders were talking like this by 1967, others were saying: "Well, we're not sure yet. Two years or three years is not enough time. We must stick it out until we're absolutely certain that we have bought enough time to stabilize areas like that." American leaders were by no means sanguine about letting Indonesia go. Indeed, they viewed Indonesia as *the* most important domino, save Japan itself.

QUESTION: It seems almost inconceivable to me that we would have paid all of the costs that you mention just because we wanted to feel good about ourselves. Why did we do it?

ANSWER: That is a terrific question. This gives me a chance to make one thing clear that time did not let me make clear in my presentation. We did not become involved in Vietnam for altruistic reasons or to make ourselves feel good. We were not motivated by a desire to hold up our hands for the television camera and say: "Mom, we're number one, we're number one." It was nothing like that at all. I think that, from the turn of the century onward, there has been a sense that while the American economy was not in the same kind of export-or-die straits as the Japanese economy, the United States could not remain a free-enterprise capitalist country without recourse to profit maximization outside the confines of the home market. My book *China Market* is concerned with the consensus on overproduction—a cardinal belief of American policymakers from the 1890s onward. Believing that the American home market could not provide an adequate rate of profit from commodity sales and capital investments, they concluded that the United States must look elsewhere. Some did argue that if we chose to establish a system of state-targeted investment, we might not have to go into Latin America or Asia or Europe to obtain outlets for our surplus capital and commodities. But American business leaders did not like notions of state-managed capital. In their minds, we could not have free enterprise in the United States without ultimately having a free world.

By 1940, the American business elite viewed prosperity as indivisible and believed that we could not be prosperous here unless we had prosperous trading partners elsewhere in the international system. Even nominally left-wing labor groups like the CIO, the Congress of Industrial Organizations, were saying the same thing by 1945, noting that World War II had seen American productivity increase tenfold and consumptive power increase much less. And they feared that the United States would plunge back into a depression unless we could revive the purchasing power of our major trading partners. The exercise of hegemony seemed to be the only way to secure the revival of the world system.

Americans looked back to the golden age of British dominance in the nineteenth century, and they concluded that only one nation, the United States, had the power and the will to force other countries to abide by a certain set of economic and political principles that would create an open universe of profit-making opportunities. American leaders were not motivated primarily by altruistic reasons. They acted initially for material reasons, and eventually for psychic rewards as well. Who wants to give up being "numero uno," even if the material circumstances change?

There was, as Senator J. William Fulbright once called it, an arrogance of power that crept into the American mind. If you take seriously the old bromide that power corrupts and absolute power corrupts absolutely, then you must be concerned by the fact that we are talking about nearly absolute power.

QUESTION: When the United States was the only country to have the bomb, we played world policeman. Do you feel that SDI is merely round two?

ANSWER: Yes, in several ways. In the obvious military sense, there may be strategic value in SDI, perhaps less for national defense than for potentially offensive uses in space. A near monopoly of that kind of system might enable the United States to perpetuate a global or galactic policeman role. That is part of it. But I do not think you should underestimate the military Keynesianism* involved in SDI. Given the fact that the United States no longer has the economic dominance that it had thirty

---

*During the Great Depression of the 1930s, British economist John Meynard Keynes argued that governments should increase their spending to compensate for the lack of business investment and consumer purchasing. His ideas about priming the economic "pump" gained widespread acceptance among American leaders when government spending on military equipment during World War II generated economic recovery in the United States.

years ago and given a sense of lost comparative advantage in a whole host of product lines that one sees in the rust belt in the Midwest and in other places in America, there is some hope, if not conviction, that SDI can be a marvelous kind of economic pump primer with technological spinoffs that will open up a new post-industrial era and renew the economic basis of hegemony. Without sustained economic power, the United States cannot play the role of world policeman. It is not possible.

Malcom Browne, an American journalist who covered the war in Vietnam, suggested in a recent article in the *New York Times* that the debate over Star Wars is a dead debate. He concluded that the United States will go forward with SDI regardless of the validity of the arguments advanced by opponents and proponents of the proposal. Whether or not SDI will work as a military system, Browne explained, it will generate somewhere between twenty and twenty-five trillion dollars in demand for private-sector goods and services.

There is another interesting side to the question. SDI could give the United States a way of managing and rationing the transfer of technology. In a free-market economy, we know that any technology we create today the Japanese are going to copy and in twelve months beat us with our own innovation. Star Wars is a way of negating some of that because in the name of security the United States can classify certain types of technology and subcontract to the Japanese or to the Germans only nonclassified things that are not the "right stuff." The American press talks about SDI only in military terms. But the German press and the Japanese press talk about SDI largely in economic terms.

QUESTION: In your view, what is the role of organizations like the World Bank and the AID Agency in global economic policy?

ANSWER: The obvious function of the World Bank or the International Monetary Fund (IMF) or AID is to create a kind of infrastructure in the rest of the world so that Americans and others, in theory at least, can profit. One of the things that both the World Bank and the IMF historically have done is force nations to choose between implementing their domestic economic programs and functioning in the world system. These institutions attempt to prevent nations from resorting to devaluation, domestic inflation, or domestic welfare programs. If countries are going to be functioning members of the world trading community and over the long run have a balanced trade in terms of exports and imports, they may be forced to impose austerity programs at home, cut back domestic spending, cut back the wage levels, and do things that will make them price-competitive so that they can be reciprocal trading partners and more or less export as much as they import. The big power of international financial agencies is the power to determine domestic economic policy. There is nothing more sovereign than the ability to make choices about how your budget is going to be written—how you are going to spend your money and how are you going to make other basic economic choices. In effect, those choices have been made indirectly for you by outside historical actors.

There is one interesting new wrinkle, which may or may not suggest a future trend. Instead of working indirectly through international organizations like IMF or the World Bank, the United States recently imposed directly a protectorate arrangement on Liberia: we said to the Liberians that we would send over American experts to write their budget, oversee their collection of taxes, oversee their central bank, and help them make a whole series of basic choices. In some ways, this is a reversion back to the more overt dollar-diplomacy practiced by the United States in Central America during the early twentieth century before the days of the Good Neighbor Policy. I do not know if this is just an aberration, an exception, or if (as some hypothesize) hegemonic powers in the midst of decline begin to do what the British did: move back to more closed systems; no longer trust their capacity to effect their will in a free-world context; begin to manipulate and play with the rules of the game; and move toward a policy of formal colonialism.

QUESTION: I notice that you did not say much about Burma, Siam, Thailand, Malaysia, Australia, and India. And I was wondering if you could say that, at the end of the Indochina struggle, the United States had won an 80-percent victory.

ANSWER: I think it is very debatable that the Vietnam War accounts for the fact that the dominoes did not fall in the way that they were supposed to fall in Southeast Asia. One can make a counterargument that if the United States had not escalated at certain points in the 1960s but instead worked for political disengagement, maybe even more of Southeast Asia would have remained free from communism. It is possible, for example, that Cambodia might not have fallen to communism had the United States not expanded the war into Cambodia under Nixon. In general, I am not certain that you can necessarily make a cause-and-effect argument and conclude that American policy in Vietnam produced any given result.

Nonetheless, I would quite agree with you that in some ways the intended purposes of the United States were served in Southeast Asia. Whether or not they might have been better served by nonmilitary policies seems to be subject to debate. But, even if we accept your 80–20-percent proposition, it begs the final issue that still confronts us today, you today and me today. And that is what were the lessons of our experience in Vietnam and what meaning do we extract from it? This question is crucial in terms of what kind of policy we are going to support and not support. Did the Vietnam War coincide with and accelerate some decline in American power and stimulate polycentric movements in the world?

QUESTION: Do you see a waning of American power or a disarray of American foreign policy during the last decade? To use your term, is this hegemonic power declining? Is there always a number one or are there periods of time when there is no number one? If there has to be a number one, are some hegemonic countries preferable to others?

ANSWER: The great French historian Fernand Braudel has argued that there is a process of centering then decentering and recentering that is perpetually going on and that it is like an organic process which in some ways cannot be avoided. One can argue that hegemony contains within it, by its very nature, the seeds of its own unraveling. Hegemony tends, for a variety of reasons, ultimately to erode the very economic base upon which it rests. Hegemonic countries tend to convert themselves over a time into *rentier* nations that live off foreign investments. They end up specializing in arms on the one hand and international finance on the other, while producing little except fast-food hamburgers at home.

As to your other concern, one has to make one's own qualitative judgments about whether or not one hegemonic power is preferable to the others. Every nation that has ever been number one always says it is the best. It takes a lot of arrogance to play that role. Hegemonic countries had better believe that they are exceptional. Certainly the British thought they were exceptional. They always said that the British Empire was more benign and more generous than other empires. But they would be hard put to persuade some people in India or Ireland or Africa that that indeed was the case. Likewise, from the day the Puritans set foot on American soil, there was a new-world sense of exceptionalism that said: "Yes, we are different, we are better."

My pitch in my own foreign-policy courses is to demystify. I do not want my students to think that the United States is necessarily worse than other nations operating in the world, that there are evil men in Washington and on Wall Street who run the world in ways that are much worse than the methods used by anybody else. I do, however, want them to question the notion that we are better than anybody else. I try to get them to accept, as an operative premise, that we are just like other folks, neither worse nor better, and that the United States operates for its own purposes in much the same way that other nation-states do. In other words, our main task is to understand how the world system works, and then we can make judgments about whether some nation-states are better or worse than others—if we still feel the need.

# INDEX

Afghanistan, 78–79
Agency for International Development (AID), 67
  role of, 104–5
America. *See* United States
Antiwar movement, 1, 23, 24–25, 31–32, 42, 83, 94
  and student deferments, 46
Asian Co-Prosperity Sphere, 89
  *See also* Greater East Asian Co-Prosperity Sphere
Association of Southeast Asian Nations (ASEAN), 49–50

Bay of Pigs (1961), 94
Braudel, Fernand, 106
Browne, Malcom, 104
Brzezinski, Zbigniew, 96
Bundy, McGeorge, 26, 96
Bunker, Ellsworth, 39
Burke, Edmund, 26

Calley, William, 78n–79n
Cambodia, 31, 105
  bombing of, 4, 25
  "secret war" in, 51, 52
Capitalism
  international quality of, 85
  preservation of, 9–10
Carter, Jimmy, 96
Case-Church Amendment, 48, 52
Castro, Fidel, 73, 93–94
Central America, 56–57, 99
  See also *individual country*
China, People's Republic of, 9
  Civil War, 88
  and international communism, 17
  Vietnamese hatred of, 3, 22
*China Market* (McCormick), 102

Churchill, Winston, 17
Clark, Ramsey, 45
Clausewitz, Karl von, 40, 43, 45, 67
Clifford, Clark, 28
Cold War, 89, 97
Colvin, John, 55
Communism
  in post-Vietnam War Southeast Asia, 9–10
  in Southeast Asia, 6, 30–31
  U.S. assumptions about, 3, 16–17
  and U.S. foreign policy, 35
  Vietnam War as challenge by, 4–6
Conflict
  grand strategy level of, 63–64, 67–70
  levels of, 61–64
  operational level of, 62, 66
  tactical level of, 61–62, 64–65
  technical level of, 61, 64
  theater strategy level of, 62–63
Congo, crisis in, 93–94
Congress of Industrial Organization (CIO), 103
Constitution, violation of, 28–29
Containment, strategy of, 40
Credibility gap, 23, 25
Cronkite, Walter, 6, 47, 49
Cuba, 93–94
  missile crisis (1962), 94
Culminating point of success, 68–70, 71
Czechoslovakia, Hitler's encroachment on, 19

Demilitarized Zone, 44
Democracy, and dissent, ix
Democratic party, effect of Vietnam War on, 24

Diem, President of South Vietnam, 19, 41, 54, 83, 84, 93
Dien Bien Phu, 5, 17
Dissent, in a democracy, ix
Dodge Plan, 86, 87
Domino theory, 9, 21, 91–92, 99, 105–6
Draft, student deferment from, 46
Dulles, John Foster, 40
Dung, General, 49

Eagleton, Thomas, 28, 33
Eden, Anthony, 17
Eisenhower, Dwight D., 3, 17, 18, 21, 22, 40, 42, 48, 54
El Salvador, 73
European Defense Community, 101

Fonda, Jane, 45
Food for Peace Program, 11
Ford, Gerald R., 52, 83
Foreign policy, and historical knowledge, 2–4, 14–15
France, 100, 101
  imperialism of, 3, 15–16, 17
  leaving NATO, 71
Fulbright, J. William, 103

Galbraith, John K., 14–15
Geneva Accords (1954), 43, 44n, 93
  *See also* Geneva Conference
Geneva Agreement on Laos (1962), 43
Geneva Conference (1954), 3, 18, 84
Grand strategy level of conflict, 63–64, 67–70
Greater East Asian Co-Prosperity Sphere, 98
  *See also* Asian Co-Prosperity Sphere
Great Society program, 42
Green Berets, 41
Guerrillas, 42, 43
Gulf of Tonkin Resolution, 26, 45

Hearden, Patrick J., xi, 1–10
Hegemony
  concept of, 8–10
  defined, 84–85
  U.S.
    erosion of, 96–97
    future of, 106–7
    post-World War II, 88–89

Helicopter, 43, 46–47
History, need for knowledge of, 14–15
Hitler, Adolf, 19
Ho Chi Minh, 3, 16, 17, 18, 19, 21, 22, 54–55
Ho Chi Minh Trail, 53
Human rights diplomacy, 97
Humphrey, Hubert, 17

Imperial presidency, 95
Indochina, in nineteenth and twentieth centuries, 15–18
Indonesia, 100, 102
International Control Commission, 43
Internationalism, 85–86, 87
International Monetary Fund (IMF), 104–5
Intervention, preconditions of (Weinberger), 74–75
Iran, 77
Iran-Contra affair, 32
Iriye, Akira, vii–ix

Japan, 9, 89–90, 91–93, 97–99, 101
  economic recovery of, 95
  and Indochina, 15–16
Johnson, Lyndon B., 5–6, 17, 18, 19, 23–24, 26–28, 31, 37, 41, 42, 45n, 47–48, 49, 55, 83, 94, 95

Kennan, George Frost, 87
Kennedy, John F., 11, 15, 18, 22, 26, 27, 40–41, 43n, 45, 54, 71, 94n
Kennedy, Paul, vii–viii
Kennedy, Robert, 24
Kent State tragedy, 25
Keynes, John Meynard, 103n
King, Martin Luther, 48
Kissinger, Henry, 55
Korean War, 42
Krushchev, Nikita, 40, 41, 94n

Laos, 31
Liberia, 105
Linear logic, 8
Luttwak, Edward N., 6–8, 61–80
  biographical sketch of, 59–60

MacArthur, Douglas, 42
MACV. *See* United States Military Assistance Command, Vietnam
Mansfield, Mike, 17

Mao Zedong, 17, 88
Marcos, Ferdinand, 29–30
Marshall Plan, 86, 87, 101
McCarthy, Eugene, 24
McCormick, Thomas J., 8–10, 83–173
  biographical sketch of, 81–82
McGovern, George S., 2–4, 13–35
  biographical sketch of, 11–12
  candidacy for president, 24, 32–33
McNamara, Robert S., 7–8, 14, 26,
  64, 65, 66, 96
Meiji Restoration, 101
*Mein Kampf* (Hitler), 19
MIAs, 33–34
Military strategy
  levels of, 7, 61–64
  rotation of officers, 7–8
Monroe Doctrine, 17
Montgomery, Sonny, 33–34
Morality, in international relations,
  2–4
Munich Conference (1938), 19
My Lai, 78, 78n–79n

Napalm, 21, 27
Nationalism, 85
National self-determination, principle of, 3
News media, 83–84
  censorship of, 47
  effect on public opinion, 6
  power of, 49, 51–52
Ngo Dinh Diem. *See* Diem, President of South Vietnam
Nicaragua, 30, 72–73
Nixon, Richard M., 4, 11, 15, 17,
  19, 24, 25, 28n, 31, 53, 55, 83,
  84, 94–95, 100, 105
North, Oliver, 29
Nuclear weapons, 27
  atomic bomb, 86
  as diplomacy, 88
  H-bomb, 89
  threat of, 42

Operational level of conflict, 7, 62, 66
Ortega, Daniel, 73

Paris Peace Agreement, 48–49
Pentagon, civilians in, 7–8
*Pentagon and the Art of War, The*
  (Luttwak), 75

Pham Van Dong, 34
Phoenix Program, 21, 51–52
Pike, Douglas, 44–45
*Platoon*, 50–51
Pol Pot, 4, 25
POWs, 33, 34
"Prussians," 97

Rayburn, Sam, 17
Reagan, Ronald, 10, 21, 29–30, 77, 96
Regionalism, policy of, 91
Reston, Scotty, 41
*Rise and Fall of the Great Powers*
  (Kennedy), vii
Rommel, Erwin, 67
Roosevelt, Franklin D., 16, 86
Rostow, Walt, 26
Rusk, Dean, 14, 18, 26, 94
Russell, Richard, 17

Sihanouk, Norodom, 25, 52
Silent majority, 100
Small war concept, 41
Somoza dynasty, 30
Southeast Asia Treaty Organization
  (SEATO), 46
Soviet Union
  and Afghanistan, 78–79
  culminating point of success,
    69–70
  and international communism, 17
  nuclear testing in 1949, 87–88
  -United States relations, 4, 22–23
Stalin, Joseph, 77–78
Star Wars. *See* Strategic Defense
  Initiative
Strategic Defense Initiative, 10, 61–
  63, 79–80, 96, 103–4
Strategy
  action and reaction in, 67–70
  misapplication of efficiency in,
    70–71
  paradoxical logic of, 69–70
Sukarno, President of Indonesia,
  100, 102
Sun Tzu, 39, 49

Tactical level of strategy, 7, 61–62,
  64–65
Tet Offensive (1968), 5, 37, 46–47,
  48, 53, 55, 76, 84, 93, 94
  media coverage of, 6

Theater level of strategy, 7, 61,
62–63, 64
Third world
development of, 89
"Prussians' " view of, 97
"Traders," 96–97
Truman, Harry S., 3, 5, 16–17, 40,
54, 83
Truman Doctrine (1947), 5, 40

United Nations, 42–43
United States
as arms supplier, 19–20
attitudes toward, and Vietnam
War, viii
commitment in Vietnam, 91
"decline" of, vii–viii
as global policeman, 99–100
as Great Britain's hegemonic
successor, 86
historical knowledge and foreign
policy, 2–4
"imperial overstretch," vii
international strategy, 6–8
public opinion in, 31–32
-Soviet relations, 4, 22–23
United States Army
officer leadership in, 65–66,
75, 77
performance in Vietnam War,
73–74
United States Military Assistance
Command, Vietnam (MACV), 37,
66, 67, 73–74

Vance, Cyrus, 96
Veterans (U.S.)
frustrations of, 20–21
and movie *Platoon*, 50–51
reaction to, 14
Vietnam psychosis, 45, 57
Vietnam War
antiwar movement. *See* Antiwar
movement
as civil war, 19

Cold War perspective of, 4–6
costs of, to U.S., vii–viii, 4
current interest in, 1–2
as deterrent to spread of communism, 30–31, 93–94, 95
effect of public opinion, 74
effect on U.S. policy, 10
favorable effects of, viii
global effects of, 9–10
historical causation, 8–10
lack of support by South Vietnamese, 57, 76
lessons of, 49–51, 74–75, 96–97
as military defeat, 7–8
and morality, 13–14
objective and strategy of, 40–43
and the passions of the people,
45–49
reasons for U.S. involvement in,
102–3
results of, 22
strategic thinking in, 64
U.S. military forces in, 43–45
"winning" of, 53–54

War
criteria of success of, 40
objective of, backed by strategy,
40–43
War Powers Act, 28–29
Watergate scandal, 25, 48, 49, 52, 84
Weapons design, post-Vietnam War,
72
Weinberger, Casper, 74–75
Wellington, Duke of, 39
Westmoreland, William C., 4–6,
28, 39–57, 64, 66, 73–74, 79
biographical sketch of, 37–38
Wilson, Woodrow, 48
Wisemen, The, 94
World Bank, role of, 104–5
World War II, leadership in, 75–76

Yom Kippur War, 48

**DATE DUE**

| MAY 10 2001 | |
| --- | --- |
| | |
| | |
| | |
| | |
| | |
| | |
| | |
| | |
| | |
| | |
| | |
| | |
| | |
| | |
| | |
| | |

GAYLORD                                    PRINTED IN U.S.A.